WITH GREAT *Mercy*

KATHY GILBERT TAYLOR

CREATION HOUSE

A STRANG COMPANY

WITH GREAT MERCY by Kathy Gilbert Taylor
Published by Creation House
A Strang Company
600 Rinehart Road
Lake Mary, Florida 32746
www.creationhouse.com

Unless otherwise noted, all Scripture quotations are from the New
King James Version of the Bible. Copyright 1979, 1980, 1982 by
Thomas Nelson, Inc., publishers. Used by permission.

Scripture quotations marked KJV are from the King James Version of
the Bible.

Cover design by Terry Clifton

Library of Congress Control Number: 2005927880
International Standard Book Number: 1-59185-850-X

05 06 07 08 09 — 987654321
Printed in the United States of America

❧ Contents ❧

*In memory of Peggy Sue Taylor,
my beloved sister-in-law,
and Susie Kuntz,
my cherished friend*

༈ Chapter 1 ༈

A Walk Through the Valley

For a mere moment I have forsaken you,
But with great mercies I will gather you.
—ISAIAH 54:7

Without warning, unexpected and unexplained electrocution-like pains violently began to course through the right side of my face and my jaw. For seven years the pain threatened my health, my career, and my personal life. My relationship with God was initially damaged. I did not blame my pain on Him, but I wanted Him to make it stop. I had been ill before, but there had always been a way to regain my health. These healings had resulted from surgery, a better diet, rest, medication, or supernatural means. This time God did not seem to be on the scene.

Sometimes the pain made speaking impossible and noise intolerable. A cool breeze on my face, brushing my teeth, and washing my face caused me to feel as though a bolt of lightening had struck the right side of my head. The pain occurred at random: waking me from a sound sleep; sitting quietly in church; receiving a gentle kiss from my husband; speaking. The extreme nature of the pain is impossible for me to describe or define fully.

My classroom, once filled with the antics and laughter that are involved with learning and teaching drama, had become a silent desert. It was occupied by a teacher who could no longer communicate her knowledge or ideas to her students. When the pains occurred during class, I tried to hide from my students. I did not want them to see the pain as it ravaged my very being. My heart was touched by my students' concern for me, yet I was dismayed by their fears for me. There were times that I crouched behind my desk, silently asking God why He had forsaken me.

I was frustrated because I did not know what I should ask God to heal.

I was plagued with uncertainties. Fear became part of my life. I was afraid I would not get relief. I was afraid I would lose my career. I was afraid my husband would not be able to cope with my disability. I wondered if I might be reaping pain and illness for my sins. Was God punishing me? I did not have the answers, but I believed, even in the midst of my harshest pains, that God does not strike us with pain and afflictions.

What I knew and still know is that Jesus came to give us abundant life. It is the enemy, not God, who steals and destroys our health and our happiness. I examined my life and realized that much had been stolen from me. In faith, I asked God to deliver me from my anguish and to restore my life. I had experienced immediate healings years before, and now I would trust God to bestow His healing grace upon me once more. Although at times I continued to feel that God had forgotten me, I would remember the promise of His faithfulness. Through God's sustaining mercy, I knew I would someday be victorious over the pain.

In a moment of overwhelming pain, have you ever felt that God had forsaken you? How has God's mercy helped you endure your own suffering?

_____

_____

_____

_____

_____

❧❦

Has anything like this happened in your days,
Or even in the days of your fathers?

—JOEL 1:2

My symptoms baffled not only my family and friends but also the medical professionals whom I visited. Because the pain seemed to originate in a tooth, I began to seek treatment from dentists and oral surgeons. Some of them told me they could not find the source of the pain. Others guessed. A few dentists and physicians told me I had temporomandibular joint disorder (TMD). It seemed incredulous that TMD was the answer. My pain was so intense that it could drive me to my knees. I knew that something about this diagnosis was amiss.

When I talked to other individuals who had been diagnosed with TMD, I realized that some of my pain and symptoms were the same. However, my other symptoms would display themselves again, and I began to grow even more confused. Many of my painful experiences were unique. No one had encountered anything like them. I felt so alone, so unsure of myself. I wondered if this pain was real. Sometimes it would disappear for almost a month. Each time it went into remission, I told myself that I could conquer it. Then unexpectedly, the pain jumped back into my face, and the cycle of agony would begin once more.

My self-confidence barely existed. I still was not sure that I really had TMD. Had I merely lost my ability to cope with the stressors of everyday life? Did I still have a grip on reality? I had barely reached my forties and feared I was having a breakdown. Yet I would not relinquish hope. For more than a year, I continued to present myself to physicians in the hope of finding relief.

I felt old and exhausted at the age of forty-one. Overnight I had changed from a healthy person to someone who was fatigued and sometimes depressed. My frustration grew. It showed on my face and resonated in my voice. My posture deteriorated; suddenly this confident person looked defeated. I did not understand why God had not healed me and why my suffering continued to increase.

3

Have you been puzzled by symptoms of your own illness? How has God helped you gain insight into the nature or cause of your infirmity?

_____

_____

_____

_____

_____

❀❀

Of obscure speech, beyond perception,
Of a stammering tongue that you cannot understand.

—ISAIAH 33:19

Disability and loss come in many different forms. No one can escape some form of loss, and sometimes loss is a consequence of a disability. From trigeminal neuralgia, I lost the ability to speak clearly and to be understood. I thank God that my speech was not affected every day. Although talking frequently hurt, the difficulty with my speech did not occur as frequently. When it did, my frustration level would soar.

On the worst of days, I could not open my mouth wide enough to speak. Sometimes my facial muscles seemed to be frozen. At other times, moving my mouth and jaw was so painful that I could hardly bear it. Difficulty swallowing also impaired my speech. When my facial nerves and muscles began to relax again, I felt so thankful just to be able to speak clearly. I did not have to be concerned when someone I did not know at the grocery store asked me where bread was located. I could give directions over the telephone to delivery personnel rather than trying to get their facsimile number or e-mail address to send written instructions. I could sing. I could make phone calls.

In the classroom, my speech presented some interesting situations. My students found humor in the fact that their teacher sounded like the cartoon character Elmer Fudd. Yet they seemed eager to come to my aid. They volunteered to read directions aloud. They offered to come to the board and help me explain a concept. They helped me laugh at the situation.

One regret I have now is that I was not more thankful for the ability to speak clearly before my disability emerged. How easy it had been for me to take speaking for granted. I know there are many things in life that I still do not recognize as blessings; it seems that I have to lose something before I realize its value. My prayer is that I can appreciate more of my blessings rather than selfishly expect what I have to remain and to want more. I believe it is fine to desire an improvement in one's standard of living; however, I think that before we want more, we should acknowledge and be thankful for what we already have.

Has a part of your body refused to function effectively? How can you show God your appreciation for blessings that remain?

_____

_____

_____

_____

_____

❧❧

I will both lie down in peace, and sleep;
For You alone, O Lord, make me dwell in safety.

—PSALM 4:8

I am thankful for the times my pain went into remission. Sometimes, several weeks would pass before the symptoms would once again strike me. During the "healthy" times, I would feel as though I could be in command of the situation. I thought that if I would just relax more, the pain would stay away. In spite of my efforts to control my pain, each recurrence would strike with pains that were stronger, longer lasting, and more debilitating. I realized I would have to rely on God even more than I had in the past, but completely surrendering to Him was something I was not ready to do.

Instead, I learned how to take refuge in my home. When I would come in from work, I would go to my bedroom to be alone for a while. I blocked noise and bright light from my sanctuary. I rediscovered my love for reading fiction. Social gatherings were no longer attractive to me. Although I had always been a gregarious person, I began to feel comfortable only in the smallest of groups.

I learned how to retreat. I was surprised by my ability to appreciate solitude because aloneness was not something that I had previously cherished. I had not married until I was in my mid-thirties, and I had experienced quite a bit of loneliness before that. I had never imagined that being alone could feel so good.

How I cherished the days in which there was no pain. They were filled with peace and activity. My frustration with God subsided with the pain, and I was able to build my faith during the calmness. I realized I had much to appreciate. I remembered that many people suffered much more than I did. I thanked God that I did not have an illness that could infect others or one that could destroy my mind. Thank You, Lord, for sheltering me in Your harbor of peace.

Have you had an hour, a day, or a week in which you had a reprieve from your symptoms? How do you find a way to dwell in God's love and safety?

_____

_____

_____

_____

_____

❧❦

Yea, though I walk through the valley of the shadow of death,
I will fear no evil; For You are with me; Your rod and
Your staff, they comfort me.

—PSALM 23:4

Finally, I received a diagnosis. On the same day, both an orthodontist and a chiropractor arrived at a more specific analysis of my illness. They directed me to the Internet so I could learn more about my disability, trigeminal neuralgia, a condition caused by a compressed blood vessel on the fifth cranial nerve. At home, I searched the Internet for valid sites on trigeminal neuralgia. Many support sites existed, and I visited several. As I read more about the condition, the empowerment that I had gained from having medical professionals recognize the source of my pain quickly began to evaporate.

As an educator, I had been trained to believe that knowledge is power. To see my symptoms listed as indications of a specific ailment initially provided me with relief. I had questioned my own experience, but reading about symptoms that clearly reflected my own suffering gave me a feeling of validation. I had the assurance that I was not alone in this experience.

Yet the more I read, the more I became aware that many individuals who had sought relief through medications and surgery had not found it. Others talked of the isolation that had been caused by the disease. I also read that the suicide rate for individuals with trigeminal neuralgia (TN) was very high. I remembered the times I had asked God to please let me die a quick death rather than to endure this pain for years to come. I thought about the times when I had felt as though I was truly in the shadow of death.

It seemed the knowledge about my condition had backfired. My feelings of empowerment quickly turned to fear. Had I only learned I was powerless in this situation? I did not understand how I could live with this illness or how I could recover. My only resource was God's promise to comfort me. God, please take this fear from me. Let my comfort and strength be a result of Your presence in my life. Lord, I cannot live through this tremendous pain without the guidance of Your rod and Your staff. Keep me close to You. Although I walk through the valley of the shadow of death, I will value and cling to the life that You have given me.

Have you ever felt as though you were in the valley of the shadow of death? What assurance do we have that God is with us during our most painful moments?

_____

_____

_____

_____

_____

❧❦❧

But those who wait on the Lord shall renew their strength;
They shall mount up with wings like eagles, They shall run and
not be weary, They shall walk and not faint.

—ISAIAH 40:31

After asking God to help me cope with the information about trigeminal neuralgia, I waited for my husband Bob to come home. I shared with him the diagnosis and the information I had learned from the Internet. His compassion and sorrow were evident. Bob reached out to me, embraced me, and encouraged me. He reminded me that God is our Healer. When medical science has nothing to offer us, hope lies in recognizing that God created science, scientists, medicine, and physicians. God would provide my healing.

I asked God for physical strength and stamina. How I wanted to mount up with wings so that I could fly away and escape the pain I bore. To receive wings of eagles, I would have to wait on the Lord. I had not been successful in previous situations that required waiting. I do everything I can to avoid a wait. I don't even like to wait for a table at a restaurant. Would I be required to learn difficult lessons just to deal with my pain? I did not want to wait! I did not want to take the time to form a deeper relationship with Christ. I just wanted those wings.

I did not have a choice, so I began to wait upon the Lord. I learned how to serve Him. I did not know what He had in store for me, but I knew it was better than what I currently had. With the encouragement of my husband, my mother, and others whom I love, I began to trust God even more for my healing. When pain was at a minimum, I used the time to garner spiritual and physical strength. I learned how to cherish and use each day to its fullest.

Over time, my standard for measuring good days changed. The wait began as a situation to be endured, but God changed it into an opportunity for me to find His mercy. I received many blessings, and through them I learned that I could sometimes focus on other issues even while the pain raged. Waiting became part of living and learning to accept God's plan instead of charging ahead with mine.

Have you had a good day or a pleasant experience recently? How has God used others to encourage you in the midst of your battle?

_____

_____

_____

_____

_____

❧❧

Disaster will come upon disaster.

—EZEKIEL 7:26

Soon, my seed of faith would encounter more adversity. Illness produced associated issues. Communicating was growing more and more difficult for me. My frustration showed in my gestures, facial expressions, and tone of voice. I became more and more sensitive to noise.

One thing that I have never liked about myself is that I show my emotions easily. I cry at sad movies. My eyes grow wide and my hands quickly find a place on my hips when I feel anger. During the time of my illness, I discovered that my supervisor did not like this aspect of my personality either. In fact, she wrote her doubts about my emotional stability on my yearly evaluation. It was in writing. I was shocked. Just being able to keep up with my workload and to cope with the pain had been an amazing feat. It was obvious that my principal did not comprehend the amount of pain I was in. Now there was a terrible blight on my employment record. Teaching drama, which had been one of my blessings in life, had become one more source of conflict.

The situation at work continued to deteriorate. Sorrow came to my best friend, Page, who taught two doors down from me. This young woman, who was still in her thirties, had become like a sister to me. She had the sweetest spirit, yet she cleverly cloaked it in a personality with a sparkling and enthusiastic sense of humor. Two years earlier, she had been diagnosed with breast cancer. The treatment had been successful, and not a trace was left.

Suddenly, Page's cancer was back, and it had metastasized in her lungs and her liver. I felt panic to my very core. I could not imagine everyday life without her. She and her husband spent a great deal of time with Bob and me. Both of them had shown compassion for my own plight. I felt as though my heart would completely break. I asked God to heal her, to give her more time. My friend and I were in our own separate wildernesses. I knew God was walking with us, but I did not "feel" as though He walked through the valley with me. I had His Word to reassure me.

His presence was a fact, not a feeling. God is always with us. I would continue to wait for the Lord's answers to my prayers.

Have you had heartbreaking news during the course of your illness? How can you ask God to intervene in the lives of your loved ones?

_____

_____

_____

_____

_____

❧❧

Fear not, for I am with you; Be not dismayed,
for I am your God. I will strengthen you, Yes, I will help you,
I will uphold you with My righteous right hand.

—ISAIAH 41:10

Although getting an initial appointment with a physician who would treat trigeminal neuralgia was difficult, I finally managed to do just that. The doctor prescribed anti-seizure medication, which is often used for the condition. At first, the medication caused me to feel terribly drowsy. As time progressed, I became more alert and considered the medication a gift from God. It kept the pain at bay.

It was not long before I found a neurologist who treated trigeminal neuralgia. Upon examining me, she discovered a skin rash, indicating that I was allergic to my medication. My physician told me not to be concerned because several new drugs were available for trigeminal neuralgia. I tried them, one by one. Each time I had an allergic reaction, but the reactions to each drug were unique. After the fourth reaction, I was at my wit's end. The physician told me she had nothing else to offer me. I asked her how I could deal with the pain, and she had no suggestions. The doctor also added that no pain medication would provide relief for my condition because the pain was too severe. My husband and I were stunned as we listened to the doctor's words.

I felt totally vulnerable. I had lived for several months now without the electrocution pains. Now what? I would have to depend completely on the Lord. Could I do it? I was not sure. I wanted to, yet I was not sure how I could depend on Him when I felt angry with Him. God had deserted me, in my opinion, because He had allowed the drug allergies to develop. Why me? I asked Him. I received no reply. I realized that I would have to let go of my anger and acknowledge my total dependence upon Him.

Soon I found a neurologist in my community who displayed empathy and understanding. I thank God for leading me to Dr. Donald Quick. Through Dr. Quick's medical supervision, I began to better understand

15

the nature of trigeminal neuralgia.

It became evident that God was my only source of healing, and I was going to need more faith. I worked through the dismay, telling God exactly how I felt about the situation. He already knew I was angry with Him. The process of telling Him about it brought in a renewal of my spirit. The anger dissolved. It is great to have a Father in Heaven who knows our needs and feelings before we have a chance to tell Him. I love the way He listens to me and loves me, regardless of my lack of faith. I love Him even more for the way He upholds me with His righteous hand.

Has fear been a part of your life since you have become ill? How has God strengthened you in the process of your treatment?

_____

_____

_____

_____

_____

❧❧

> For if what is passing away was glorious,
> what remains is much more glorious.
>
> —2 CORINTHIANS 3:11

Loss blossomed from a situation into a season. Some situations were easier to accept than others. My grandmother, who was eighty-five, passed from this life into eternity. Granny had been a Christian since her early adulthood. She had "that old-time religion" that people sing about. Just hours before she slipped away, my grandmother joined the crowd of loved-ones who had gathered in her hospital room in a song, "I'll Fly Away." She had not been able to eat or drink anything for days, but that did not prevent her from rising up with strength from God in her final hours. She sat up in her hospital bed, her arms lifted in the air, and sang from her heart. She praised God. That was the last thing Granny did on this earth.

Three months later, I said good-bye to Page. She died on the first day of summer vacation. My intention was to spend a great deal of time with her during the summer. During the school year, I was so depleted after teaching that I came home to rest. My guilt and loss—because I had not gone to spend time with Page after work—was sometimes overwhelming. I have thought so much about how I missed spending time with Page. I cannot reverse my decisions or actions. For those of us who have been ill, we understand that disease limits a person's energy and imposes limitations. I hope Page realized that all I could do at the time was to sustain myself.

I returned to school in the fall, but I was absent almost as much as I was there. I spent nights unable to sleep because of pain. I would go to my computer in the early hours of the morning to create alternate lesson plans for a substitute teacher and send them into school via facsimile. In the first week of December, my physician advised me to take medical leave. In one sense, I was very relieved. My body was refusing to continue at the required pace. Although I decided to follow Dr. Quick's advice, I secretly second-guessed the decision. I had lost my connection to the community. I missed my students.

In spite of the losses, my body began to garner strength. Gradually, I realized that I still had much to offer others. I became a Guardian ad Litem, and I had enough energy to begin to attend church regularly. My husband and I also became mentors for some children who were in foster care.

The love I felt for Granny and Page has never died. I have realized that I never really lost them and cherish memories of them. Many of my former students called, and some of them have visited. My husband hired a couple of them to work for him. Although Granny is not here, I have become closer to other relatives now. God always gives us enough love. He fills our paths with blessings as we continue on life's journey.

Have your losses seemed to multiply? What is something glorious that remains in your life?

_____

_____

_____

_____

_____

✥

Chapter 2

Refuge in His Wings

Be merciful to me, O God, be merciful to me! For my soul trusts
in you; And in the shadow of Your wings I will make my refuge,
Until these calamities have passed by.

—PSALM 57:1

As my journey toward finding God's mercy continued, I found
another reason to seek His refuge. My husband, who is one of the
most energetic individuals I have met, was diagnosed with a precancer-
ous tumor in his colon. When we heard the news, we felt anxious but
were thankful because the situation was not worse.

We had to go out of town for the surgery, so I took some time away
from work. The morning of the surgery came, and I went down with
Bob for his preoperative treatment. A physician came into the room and
administered an intravenous drug for nausea, and then he left. Immediately, my husband began to have a negative reaction from the drug. He
could not breathe. I watched as his entire chest wall turned red. I was
frightened beyond words. As the doctors came to attend him, I asked
God to spare Bob from harm. I stood by as the physicians discussed the
possible causes of my husband's reaction. Then I was ushered away.

The families of other patients in the area came to my side, asking me
how they could help me. Then the leader of the medical team called me
aside for a chat. It was days later before he conceded that my husband
had indeed had an allergic reaction to a drug. Bob underwent several
tests to determine if his heart had been the source of the problem or if
the episode had been a reaction to the medication. Then he was released
because he was too weak for surgery.

I do not remember where the chapel was in that huge hospital. Nor
do I remember how it looked. I just remember being alone with God.
My mother and some friends came to be with me. I had support, but I
did not have peace. It took a while to get it. I talked to God about how

inadequate I was because of my own health. The stress and lack of sleep had caused another episode of trigeminal neuralgia. After it passed, Bob went back in for surgery. Once again, things did not go smoothly, but when Bob left the hospital, he was doing well. It was good to have his illness resolved.

When I remember this time, I am reminded about the need for my quiet times with God. I need to step away from the hustle and bustle so I can feel His presence in a more powerful way. We have to be close to God in order to be in His shadow. Although He helps us in our emergencies, He wants to be involved in our daily lives. This situation helped me understand that God was there to protect me, but I needed to move closer to Him so I could trust in His protection more fully.

Have you felt as though you needed God's protection? What circumstance has led you to trust in God's refuge?

_____

_____

_____

_____

_____

❈❈

According to Your mercy remember me,
For Your goodness' sake, O Lord.

—PSALM 25:7

I am thankful that God's mercy is infinite. Many of His blessings are delivered to us through others. My mother has been His instrument more times than I can remember. Her love and faith have enriched my life. I am grateful to have a mother who has prayed for me and loved me regardless of my actions or our circumstances. Through adversity, my mother and I have forged a powerful bond and a strong friendship.

The Bible teaches us that God will give us the desires of our hearts. One of my strongest desires was at last fulfilled. My mother moved to the same town in which I lived with my husband. In fact, she bought property in our neighborhood. While sharing a neighborhood might be too close for some families, it has worked out perfectly for us. God knew how much I would need to have my mother close by, and He made a way for her to be with me.

If I had ever known how much I was really going to need my mother, I would have been terribly frightened. Because I was unaware of my approaching walk through the valley of illness, I focused on the enjoyment that would come from having her companionship. Mom was still young and active, and we enjoyed doing many of the same things. Although we do not know what the future has in store for us, God prepares a way for us to receive His goodness and mercy. Since my mother has moved here, we have thoroughly enjoyed each other's company. On my good days, we have the most delightful of times.

What matters most, though, is what my mother has done on my difficult days. She has prayed for me without ceasing, she has cleaned my home, and prepared food for my husband and me. My mother has gone to the grocery store for us and has accompanied me to medical appointments in the local area as well as out of state. She has accomplished these activities without complaint, expecting nothing in return. Her gentleness and love have been a testimony of God's faithfulness and His mercy.

When I was younger, I wanted so desperately to see the future, but I am so glad that I did not foresee this illness. I have learned that it is better to trust my future to God. From His abundant heart, He will prepare a way to meet our needs before we are aware that the need exists.

Have you wondered if God remembers your needs? How has He demonstrated His mercy and goodness in your life?

_____

_____

_____

_____

_____

❧❧

He breaks me with wound upon wound;
He runs at me like a warrior.

—JOB 16:14

When I inquired about surgical procedures regarding my condition, my neurologist referred me to the Mayo Clinic. I was blessed to have two doctors who cared about their patients, viewing them as real humans who had emotions, families, and fears. One day when I was visiting my neurologist at Mayo, I told him that it felt as though something was wrong with my jaw. He examined my neck and agreed. He referred me to a dentist, also a Christian, in another city.

I drove to Lakeland, Florida, filled with apprehension, to visit the dentist. I liked this man; he was very straightforward yet gentle. "Your situation is very grave, but there is hope." I will never forget his words. I could not believe what I had heard. How could a jaw be a grave situation? I had seen so many dentists, and none had really offered a treatment for TMD. I had actually forgotten about the diagnosis once I was told I had trigeminal neuralgia. I was brought back to the reality as the dentist explained how the TMD had progressed into my shoulder. I was told by the dentist that if untreated, it would travel farther down the right side of my body, the same side that had the compressed trigeminal nerve.

The dentist told me that he knew his limitations; he would not be able to help me. He said that he would consult with another dentist in Minnesota because he believed my situation required the greatest expertise. I could not believe his words. How could God let this happen? I was so confused, so I asked the dentist if I had TMD. He confirmed that I did. Then I replied: "So I do not have trigeminal neuralgia!"

"You have both," the dentist told me. I thought my world was going to cave in. How could I battle both of these illnesses that were attacking the right side of my head? I remembered that God had promised not to give us more than we could bear. God certainly knew me better than I knew myself because I never thought I would be able to endure the reality of this news. God knows us all better than we know ourselves. When the

23

enemy comes at us, God has already equipped us with His armor. All we have to do is reach out for it. We have to remember that the attacks are not from God but from the enemy. Wounds are frightening, but God heals our fear as well as our wounds. He is with us, and He loves us. He walks beside us and fights our battles for us.

Has your illness grown more complicated than you expected? What provisions has God made to help you win your battle?

_____

_____

_____

_____

_____

❧❧

I cried out to the Lord because of my affliction,
And He answered me.

—JONAH 2:2

Although I initially felt overwhelmed by the news I had been given about my jaw, I began to see that God was helping me on my path to wellness. I spoke with the dentist in Minnesota via telephone several times, and I felt comfortable with him and his staff before I began my journey. My friend, Dorothy, and I made reservations to leave our warm homes in Florida to travel to Minnesota in early January.

I love how God answers prayer. His answers are unique and surprising. It is true that I did not want to go to Minnesota, but I had always wanted to go to the Mall of America. Although shopping is not one of my favorite pastimes, the Mall of America was something I could not resist. Dorothy and I had a weeklong adventure. We took taxis, busses, and the hotel's van to the dentist and to the Mall of America. Sometimes we walked in the snow across the street to eat.

For two years, I traveled to Minnesota on a regular basis. Sometimes I took someone with me, and other times I went alone. My dentist molded sets of prostheses to bring my jaw into alignment. The trips placed quite a bit of stress on my trigeminal nerve. Flying was a terribly painful experience because of my misaligned bones; they affected my ear and my balance. The Minnesota cold threatened to strike my trigeminal nerve, but every time I went, God gave me a reprieve. I wrapped up my face, but the cold air never even hurt my face. Isn't this a miracle? A cool breeze in Florida would cause great pain, yet God spared me from electrocution pains when I had to encounter the bitter cold.

Our Lord really protects us from carrying more than we can handle. By the end of this very successful medical treatment, I had grown to love the people and land of Minnesota. I had grown spiritually and emotionally by traveling out of my comfort zone. Occasionally I still hear from the dentist's office. God answered my prayer; the pain that was a direct result of the TMD was gone. New friends had been made. My faith had increased.

Has an unexpected situation occurred? How did God help you put your faith in motion?

_____

_____

_____

_____

_____

❀❀

A time to tear, And a time to sew;
A time to keep silence, And a time to speak.

—ECCLESIASTES 3:7

There are a very few times when I find myself speechless; however, a call from a nurse at Mayo Clinic's dermatology department affected me this way. Most of us have had an experience in which words to describe our feelings are not available. This was one of those times. Just before one of my trips to Minnesota, I felt a nagging itch on my face. It came from a little bubble of skin. When I saw my dermatologist, he told me that it was most likely basal cell carcinoma. He took a biopsy. This was not my first skin biopsy since I had begun taking so much medication, and I was not concerned. My skin biopsies had always been negative before, and had indicated drug allergies. I dismissed this episode without considering that my dermatologist had not mentioned the possibility of skin cancer when he took the other biopsies.

I was sitting at my computer when the call from Mayo came. My mother was with me but in another room. She heard me crying, and came to see what was wrong. I pulled myself together and gave her the information. The spot on my face was skin cancer. Oh how angry I was with God! Three times now my face and head and been attacked: jaw pain; facial and cranial pain; and now the skin on my face. I asked God why these infirmities were all attacking the same area. I did not get an answer. Perhaps I was too angry to listen for one. I told my best friends about my situation, but my anger did not impress them. They saw this as the least of my issues and could not understand why I was upset about a simple form of skin cancer. Meanwhile I felt that my face had become a target for adversity. Yes, I was angry.

To remove the spot of cancer, I underwent a simple outpatient surgical procedure at Mayo. It went very well. Because the carcinoma was very close to my eye, I had to rest for a few days. In spite of the initial swelling, the scar has healed beautifully. Now every time I see it, I am reminded of my surgeon's skills. I remember that the surgeon ripped my flesh open, excised the cancer, and sewed my skin back together. I remember that God was with the surgeon and with me. The scar is insignificant; with powder on my face, it is difficult to see.

Eventually, I confessed to God my shame about my pettiness in this situation. I had complained thoroughly about something that was quite trivial. *The cancer was on the left side of my face, not the right side.* Had it been on the right side, it could have triggered an unbearable episode of trigeminal neuralgia. Yet I had dismissed this important fact because I had made a decision to be angry with God. It had been a time to stay silent rather than to complain to my friends. It had been a time to put vanity aside and to be thankful rather than gloomy. In retrospect, I realize it had been a situation in which God taught me how to put situations in proper perspective.

Have you felt anger toward God because of your illness? In what situation has God helped you to determine whether it was appropriate to stay silent or to speak?

_____

_____

_____

_____

_____

Not with eyeservice, as men-pleasers, but as bondservants of
Christ, doing the will of God from the heart.

—EPHESIANS 6:6

My body continued to mend, and my desire to have a purposeful career resurfaced. I have so much to be thankful for in my life. When I was young and needed guidance and support, many people reached out to me and saw me through a difficult time. I will never forget the people who took me under their wings. Through teaching, I had an avenue in which I could offer the same to youth who needed it. At church, I was seeing some of my former students on a regular basis. God was supplying my needs. I was grateful for His mercy.

As time progressed, I felt that I could offer more time and love to children who were in need of a family. My husband and I decided to become foster parents. Because of my fragile health, we took only one child at a time. God blessed us as the children, one by one, came in to and left our home. Our hearts could endure only a few good-byes, and our days as foster parents came to a close.

I still felt that God had something for me to do. I did not want to stay at home forever. Surely God would heal me, and I would be able to work again. I prayed and searched my heart. What I really wanted to do was to go back to school. I knew that in order to do this I would have to receive the Lord's blessing. This was something that I wanted to do. God had not asked it of me. Slowly, I began to pursue a master's degree, starting with one course at a time. It seemed impossible. The commute each way was more than an hour. Classes were three hours long. I could not do it without God's help.

My husband and others close to me voiced their loving concern about my attempt to tackle such a project. I was working for God, but I still had fears. My ability to concentrate was waning. An educator at heart, I believed that an endeavor in formal learning might help my mind regain its acuity. I took several courses before deciding on a major. A specialized field of counseling seemed just right for me.

I believed I could give back to God and to others if I were able to work with individuals who have disabilities. Through my own experience, I knew the ins and outs of illness and the changes that an illness forces one to make. This course of study seemed to be a lifeboat, a way to become a helper again rather than just one who needs help. That is what I wanted, to step back into the role of helper. I began a new path, believing that one day I would return to work and be able to assist those whom God would put in my path.

Have you ever wondered what God's will for your life is? From your heart, what can you do as a servant of Christ?

_____

_____

_____

_____

_____

❧❧

He comes from the north as golden splendor;
With God is awesome majesty.

—JOB 37:22

An exciting opportunity presented itself to my husband and me. Bob would be able to earn continuing education credits needed for his profession while on a cruise to Alaska. Although he would have to spend some time in class as the cruise was underway, he would have enough free time to tour the sites with me.

Neither of us had previously taken an overnight cruise nor had we ever been to Alaska. For many years, it had been my number one choice for a vacation. I have always been intrigued by the scenery, and I love to watch documentaries and movies filmed in Alaska. I discussed the opportunity with Dr. Quick. Because my health was continuing to improve, my doctor expressed confidence in my ability to tolerate an Alaskan vacation during the warm month of August. Bob and I had not been on a vacation in years, and now we were preparing to visit paradise.

I will never forget the unadulterated splendor of Alaska. Both Bob and I appreciated the majesty of the glaciers, the water, and the mountains. At one point, a glacier was right outside our balcony. Even on the coolest day, I was able to view the glaciers and the mountains through the ballroom of the ship. I was protected from the cold without sacrificing an opportunity to relish the scenery.

While Bob signed up for some of the more adventurous outings, I rested, read a book, or just appreciated the majesty of our surroundings. I thanked God for creating such beauty and for giving us the opportunity to see it. I also thanked Him for a time when the weather in this northern haven was mild enough for me to visit it without having pain. As I noticed how the sun created a glow from the ice-capped mountains, I thought of heaven. I know that if God has placed this much beauty on earth, I will not be able to comprehend the beauty of heaven until I reach eternity. How I long for the day when we will live with God in His glory.

Have you had an opportunity to visit an area that fills you with God's peace? What promise does God's creative handiwork hold for those who have accepted Him as their Savior?

_____

_____

_____

_____

_____

❧❧

A sower went out to sow his seed. And as he sowed,
some fell by the wayside; and it was trampled down,
and the birds of the air devoured it.

—LUKE 8:5

The day that we returned from Alaska was the first day of the new semester. I was encouraged that my health would continue to improve. I went back for more education with the belief that I could improve the lives of others as well my own. I was grateful that God had helped me form a goal: to return to work so that I could help others who had experienced illness. As I returned to school, I began to notice the fear that lived deep within my being. I was afraid of failure. Perhaps my grades would not be good enough. I had jumped out of my field—English and drama—and into health counseling.

I was not sure I would be able to learn the new material or to endure the commute. I had been isolated from others for quite a while. I felt very insecure about presenting myself to younger students who had more energy and better health. I had lost my place in the classroom. How would I adjust to being a student rather than a teacher? And there was always a chance that my trigeminal nerve would not tolerate the pace.

I stumbled my way through the summer courses. I had to make a trip to Minnesota, but it did not interfere with school. God poured out His blessings on me as I made an earnest effort to sow the seed of knowledge. It seemed that some of the world's kindest people were in this counseling field, and my classmates had been very sweet to me. The world began to look bright again. I believed that I had a future.

One day I was approached by someone who had quite a bit of authority over me. He questioned my suitability for the profession. He also stated that I lacked empathy for others. I cannot remember feeling more crushed. It was as though every cell in my body had sounded an alarm. I felt so shocked that I could not respond appropriately. I did not know what to do. I wanted to quit school. Why continue a program for which I was not suited? I felt as though my seeds of knowledge had fallen onto a wasteland, devoured by someone's words.

I was afraid to talk to classmates because he had voiced concern about their opinions of me. I remembered the old Gospel song, "Where Could I Go But to the Lord?" I reached out to God for comfort. His loving Spirit soothed me. I spoke to my mother, my husband, and long-term friends. They encouraged me. I would continue to sow.

Have you attempted to begin something new since you became ill? How has God upheld you through disappointments and frustrations?

_____

_____

_____

_____

_____

❧❦

The heavens and earth will shake;
But the Lord will be a shelter for His people.

—JOEL 3:16

For weeks, my self-confidence was shaken. Although I had support from my family and friends, I dreaded each weekly encounter with the university executive who had spoken so harshly to me. I also felt uncomfortable with my classmates. I was even wary of my peers who had been friendly and caring. I wondered if they had complained to this individual about me. Were they being kind to my face and critical when I was not present? I remembered the concerns this official had voiced regarding how my peers viewed me. I desperately wanted to talk to a classmate about this, but I could not bring myself to do it. My self-doubts had risen to the point where I was afraid of what kind of feedback I might receive.

I gave this situation to the Lord over and over again in prayer. I prayed for the person who had spoken these words to me. I asked God to bless him, and God blessed me. He gave me a special love for this individual. It was special because I could not have done it on my own. My inclination was to feel hatred. This person had no regard for the pain I had suffered or for the fact that I was newly adjusting to social situations again. In class and with my peers, I was a bundle of nervous energy. When I allow myself to get into this state, I behave one way: I talk.

In spite of the fact that talking could trigger the trigeminal neuralgia, I talked, talked, and talked. I know how turned-off I can become when I am in a class with someone who monopolizes the conversation. Now I was doing what I did not like and could not find a way to stop the behavior. Then God made a way for me to tell someone at school about the issue. I received tremendous support, and that support grew. It kept growing. Each week, I encountered hostility from the individual who had delivered the disparaging remarks, yet God sheltered me with His love in the midst of it. He gave me the assurance that I needed so that I could continue in the program.

One of my favorite songs is Dottie Rambo's "Sheltered in the Arms of God." I listen to it almost every day. My Aunt Brenda sometimes sings it at church, and each time I am marvelously blessed. The song reminds me that God is present in the midst of my life's storms. When my physical and emotional being quake with pain and fear, God steps in and provides me with His shelter. The Lord's shelter is perfect, and it thoroughly calms me. As I use my faith to step into His shelter, peace begins to flow through my spirit, my soul. It does not matter what type of storm it is—fear, pain, confusion, or sorrow—God has a shelter designed just for that situation. I am so happy to be a child of God. The knowledge that I am sheltered in His arms is a profound fact, and it is more valuable to me than anything I could learn outside God's Word.

Have you felt as though your world was totally shaken? How can you find the peace that only God's shelter can provide?

_____

_____

_____

_____

_____

Chapter 3

Lifting Up My Eyes

I will lift up my eyes to the hills—From whence comes my help?
—PSALM 121:1

Good things were happening once again. My dentist in Minnesota, Dr. Terrance Spahl, said that I was ready to complete my treatment. This meant that I would no longer have to wear my prostheses, but it also meant that I needed eight crowns. I had carefully timed this appointment for mid-November. I would have a break at school, allowing me to rest. I would return to Minnesota to receive the permanent crowns in early December, after I had taken my finals.

I had never had a tooth crowned and did not know what to expect. When I told my friends that all eight would be done at the same time, I heard gasps and sighs. They told me that one crown took a whole afternoon. How could I get all eight done in the same amount of time? I had no answers for them. All I knew is that I was ready for the temporary crowns. My neurologist prepared me for the pain that this would cause; it would directly impact my trigeminal nerve.

I tried not to be frightened, but I was. My husband, Bob, was going to make the trip with me. Our pastor, Bob Bronkema, came over to pray for me before we left. He read Psalm 121, and I understood why he had chosen it for this situation. I meditated upon God's Word, and I prayed for courage. I prayed that I would be able to endure the pain. I knew God was with me. When the day of my appointment came, however, my dentist sensed my fear. In spite of my faith, I had not been able to resolve it. My dentist arranged my chair so that I could see the vista outside. How beautiful Minnesota is in the fall.

Dr. Spahl asked me to look up at the hills that were so grandly displayed through his office window. Then he assured me that God, who had made those hills, had also made me and was able to bring me through this experience. He talked about the beauty and strength of God. He referred to the very same passage that our minister had read before we left Florida. It was not a coincidence or an accident. It was God's reassurance. Tears came to my eyes because I was so thankful that God does not give up on us when we doubt Him. After the eight temporary crowns were accomplished that afternoon, my dentist drove Bob and me back to our hotel. We took a scenic route, exploring the hills I had seen from the dentist's chair. I knew from where my strength had come. God, who formed the hills, which held the promise of His peace, had protected me through my pain and fear.

Have you received a blessing from God that could not be dismissed as a coincidence? What situation has God brought you through in spite of your doubts?

_____

_____

_____

_____

_____

৯৪৯

He will not allow your foot to be moved;
He who keeps you will not slumber.

—PSALM 121:3

This Psalm continued to uphold me. It was not until after I returned home to Florida that the pain arrived. God tells us that He will not give us more than we can handle, and it seems that the pain I experienced when I got home would have been more than I could have handled while I traveled and combated the cold weather.

Finals were quickly approaching, and I did not know how I would be able to concentrate on the material the tests would cover. I had begun to take a different type of anti-seizure medication, and it seemed to be helping. Because the pain was so severe, I visited my doctor. He increased the dosage of the anti-seizure medication. My concentration abilities seemed to grow even worse because the medication affected my central nervous system. I felt like a zombie. I asked my doctor if I would be able to concentrate to take my tests if I continued to stay on a higher dosage. He answered my question with a question: "Will you be able to effectively study with this level of pain?" I knew he had a point.

There seemed to be no answer. Between the pain and the medication, God seemed very distant. I cried and cried, frightened once more about my situation. Where was God? Soon the day came when my counseling partner and I had to tape our counseling sessions for our professor to grade. I looked forward to the chance to tell my predicament to Stephanie, my wonderful friend and classmate. On the other hand, I was very unsure about pulling myself together to act as her counselor. We decided to have me in the role of the counselor at the beginning of our session. I was afraid that once I allowed her to counsel me that I would not be able to concentrate well enough to guide Stephanie through her session.

God, who had seemed so far, distant, and unapproachable, began to seem closer as I proceeded to counsel Stephanie. He held me steadfast, and I was amazed that I could use the counseling skills I had just learned. When it was Stephanie's turn to counsel me, I found myself telling her my fears about the treatment, the pain, and finals. God has given Stephanie wonderful gifts, and counseling is one of them. He used her to help me find the strength and encouragement I needed to continue studying for finals. I received As on both final exams as well as for the final grade for both courses. I had made three trips to Minnesota that semester, and God had remained faithful to me. While He seemed distant at times, I realized that He was right there. Where? With me, as I stood firmly in the palm of His great hand.

Do you have a recurring fear? In what situation has God helped you remain steady in the midst of a discouraging situation?

_____

_____

_____

_____

_____

❧❧

And the peace of God, which surpasses all understanding, will
guard your hearts and minds through Christ Jesus.

—PHILIPPIANS 4:7

I was on my way back to Minnesota for my final appointment with
Dr. Spahl. My friend Mary Ann was with me. She had taken vacation time from work to go with me. Just a couple of hours after our
arrival, I was in the dentist's chair again. This time the fear was not present as my dentist began to put on the eight permanent crowns. When
the pain got to be more than I could tolerate, Mary Ann walked across
the street in the snow to buy my favorite soft drink for me. I drank it
and took some pain medication. Twenty minutes later, I was ready to
continue. The next thing I knew, it was done. Two years of work had
culminated in my having a new jawline. It not only eased my pain but it
also improved my appearance.

This last trip was special for so many reasons. I had become very
fond of my dentist and his staff, and I did not know if I would see them
again. God had helped me to thoroughly trust them. I had made the trip
so many times that it had become routine. When Mary Ann stopped to
view an airport monitor to determine our next step, she quickly learned
I already knew it. Mary Ann and I got to see the nicest parts of the city,
dine in the best restaurants, and shop at the best places. I already knew
these places, and now I had the joy of sharing them with her. I took time
out to rest every afternoon, and then we would be ready to go out to
dinner. This excursion seemed more like a mini-vacation rather than a
trip for medical treatment.

Perhaps the most endearing thing about this last trip is that Mary
Ann volunteered to brave the Minnesota cold with me in December.
A Bostonian, she had moved to Florida many years before because she
detests cold weather. We waited for a bus, bundled up. We have a picture
of me that shows my entire face wrapped up except my eyes. Once again,
God protected me during my trip, delaying the pain until my return
home. I thank God for Mary Ann's generosity and loyalty. As I left my

new friends in Minnesota, I had one dear friend who would return home with me and would assist me with all my needs. I thank God for the peace He gave me in closing this chapter of my life. I only hope that one day I can see my Minnesota friends once more.

This journey was similar to the one that I am on with my Lord and Savior. I have had to endure pain, but God has seen me through. I have had fears about my path, but He gave me peace. Not only did I have Him walking beside me, but I also had a human companion who was concerned about my needs and placed them above her own.

Have you had an experience that went much more smoothly than you anticipated? How has God guarded your heart and mind as you encountered an uncomfortable situation?

_____

_____

_____

_____

_____

❧❧

You have turned for me my mourning into dancing; You have put
off my sackcloth and clothed me with gladness.

—PSALM 30:11

The break between semesters lasted five weeks, spreading over December and January. I had time to mend, and my life became very peaceful. Independently of each other, both my mother and I gained a sense of assurance from God that I was healed. In early January, my strength returned. I felt that nothing could stop me. I started thinking about ways that I could complete my master's degree at a faster pace.

As the new semester began, I began a counseling practicum at the local community college. What a marvelous opportunity this was for me. The office was centrally located, and I saw plenty of former drama and journalism students. I knew that God was helping me with closure. Because I had left teaching abruptly, I had not had a chance to say good-bye to my students. Now I was saying hello to them and rebuilding relationships.

My daughter Kelli—whom I refuse to call my stepdaughter—was soon to be married. Kelli was working full-time and taking classes to work on a second degree. Because she was so busy, I had the pleasure of doing preliminary shopping. I reported my findings to Kelli so she could make the final decisions. She had asked me to serve as mother of the bride, and I was basking in this honor as well as my pain-free life. The wedding came, and it proved to be a glorious time. I thank God that Kelli married a young man whose love for her is strong, genuine, and evident.

My healing continued, and I began to exercise more. My body was getting stronger and stronger. January and February were full of opportunities to celebrate my healing, Kelli's wedding, and my hope for my future. The hope spread into March. My calendar was full. God's love and mercy had turned my sorrow into gladness. I had never been happier, and I thanked God for renewing me.

Do you have a situation in your life that is worthy of celebration? What opportunity for gladness has God given you?

_____

_____

_____

_____

_____

❧❧

If you have run with the footmen, and they have wearied you,
Then how can you contend with horses? And if in the land of
peace, In which you trusted, they wearied you, Then how will you
do in the floodplain of the Jordan?

—JEREMIAH 12:5

My pace had grown much quicker. Life was fuller than it had been in years, and my independence and self-confidence had grown immensely. At school, I was enrolled in a group counseling course and in a counseling practicum. I was the co-president of our student organization. At church, I was a youth director. I had prayed earnestly for friends, and God had provided them. Bob and I were having a social life once again.

At the end of January, I decided to take a break from youth group until March. I needed to devote my free time to wedding details. I picked up the pace with my exercise. For approximately an hour after each session, I felt rejuvenated. Then the tired feeling always came back.

Spring break came in March. I knew this would give me a chance to rest and relax. Bob and I made a trip to a local getaway: no radio, no television, just beach and tranquility. My energy continued to wane. I talked to God a little bit about this, but I was afraid to devote a lot of prayer to the situation. I knew I had been healed. I did not want to voice doubt or dismay. By the end of spring break, I was completely exhausted. I looked exhausted. My friends mentioned the fact that my exhaustion was obvious. I could see concern in their eyes. I heard it in their voices.

I wondered how I would be able to keep up with a full-time life. I could do it, I told myself. I still had no pain. Life could not be better, I openly confessed. I was not going to allow the increases God had given me to slip away. Because I believe that negative thoughts are like poison, I refused to entertain them. I was still in the process of healing. Determined to complete my race, finish my degree, and return to work, I continued toward my goals.

Have you experienced a lack of energy? How has God helped you continue in your race?

_____

_____

_____

_____

_____

ॐॐ

At this also my heart trembles, And leaps from it place.

—Job 37:1

Still trying to build my stamina, one Friday morning I was exercising at a women's center with my mother. I was doing my favorite exercise when I felt something like a bolt of lightening charge through the right side of my face. The pain astonished me. I froze in place, but no one seemed to notice. Telling myself this was just a fluke, I proceeded to another exercise station. I was almost done, and I did not tell anyone about the pain. Later that day, I wanted to talk to God about it, but I was afraid to. I was in denial about the situation, the possibility of another attack, and I did not know how to deal with it. I would not let my health slip away. I refused to believe that debilitating pain could so easily crash into my life again.

If I had been walking closer with God, I would have thrown myself at His feet for mercy. I would have asked Him to prepare me for spiritual battle. I would also have asked Him to make me a mighty prayer warrior. Instead, I ran from Him in my confusion. I was afraid to admit defeat to Him. Once again, I wondered if God might be punishing me. We had planned to have company that weekend, and as it progressed, so did the fiery pain in the right side of my face and head. I could do nothing but rest in bed.

My very existence had been threatened. I thought that with God's help, I had pulled myself out of the fire. Yet the fire was back, and I was more frightened than ever. My husband was very loving. My mother looked as though her very heart would break. I heard more love in Kelli's voice than I ever imagined. My support system was intact, but my belief that God had healed me was quickly wavering.

Have symptoms from your illness frightened you? How does God reassure you when you feel your faith waning?

_____

_____

_____

_____

_____

༄༅

Chapter 4

The Good Fight of Faith

Fight the good fight of faith, lay hold on eternal life,
to which you were also called and have confessed
the good confession in the presence of many witnesses.
—1 Timothy 6:12

As the semester closed, my pain was frequent and intense. I began to resent school, especially the commute. Part of the resentment stemmed from fear that I would not be able to continue. Summer school began almost immediately after the spring semester concluded. I thought about taking a break from school. Because many of the courses for my program are offered only once a year, I wanted to continue. I did not want to delay graduation.

God provided me with everything I needed to get through the spring and summer. Sometimes I was not able to drive for a month or more, but I had plenty of help with transportation. Bob or one of his employees drove me to the university. Other times, my friend Susie drove from another city to take me to school. Her drive was two hours each way when she did this for me. Susie also has a disability and is in pain much of the time. In spite of her pain, she embraces opportunities to give help to others, and she has been a tremendous blessing in my life. I treasure her friendship.

During this summer, I began to learn about the fight of faith. At first, I resisted the entire concept because I do not like to fight. I do not mind a confrontation to resolve issues, but after a fight I feel depleted. In spite of my disdain for fighting, I realized I had no choice. I needed relief from the pain. It was the only way I could get my life back. It was the only way I could stay in my academic program. Summer school was two days a week instead of one. My pace would have to increase rather than relax. God was merciful. When it was time for class, He gave me the energy to get there. On the days that I did not have class, I would wrestle with my pain. Comprehending my studies was difficult, but I did not want to give up.

I felt as though I was barely hanging on. I needed more from God. I needed more from myself than a confession of faith. To say that I was healed was so much easier when there had been no pain. I had become overwhelmed by the pace of school, and I did not seem to have the time or energy to invest in a closer relationship with God. How could I reprioritize? Only God could show me how.

Have you ever felt that you were involved in a fight while coping with your illness? What has God provided to help you in your battle?

_____

_____

_____

_____

_____

ఛఱఛ

For we do not wrestle against flesh and blood,
but against principalities, against powers, against the rulers
of the darkness of this age, against spiritual hosts
of wickedness in the heavenly places.

—EPHESIANS 6:12

Soon God would show me that I was dealing with more than an illness. I learned whom I was fighting and why. Through this verse, I realized the type of battle in which I was engaged. Wrestling is done at close range. It is personal. The opponents get shoved, smashed, and thrown around. It has never been a sport that I have enjoyed. Now it was not just a sport but the key to my survival and victory. All my life I had heard of spiritual warfare. I had never given a lot of thought to how much this principle could apply to physical pain and illness. When I had encountered trials, scriptures that referred to spiritual warfare had reassured and guided me.

I now have become more aware that my struggle is with spiritual forces and powers that oppose God. Whatever I face might be new for me, but the type of battle in which I am engaged is really a mere extension of the war Satan chose to wage with God long ago. Just as God uses people to bless and help others, Satan uses people to inflict emotional and physical pain on others.

God sent me help on regular basis. Faithfully, my mother came over to pray for me. As our faith and determination to win this battle grew, something odd began to happen. During our prayer time, terrible pains would hit me. I would feel worse than I had before we had started praying. The pains were so terrible that I would loudly cry out. This was difficult for me to understand. I knew God was in control. I asked how could this happen when I was praying.

I am not an expert on theology or spiritual warfare. The time had come, though, for me to find the answer to my plight. I considered the possibility that my physical pain was a direct attack from the enemy. At times, the very idea of it seemed incredulous. I resisted this idea, but

51

soon I realized that the power of the enemy was manifesting itself in my body as pain. I prayed. I read my Bible. I discovered that Satan has tremendous power; he and his fallen angels try to destroy people's lives through physical and other types of pain. The battle continued.

Have you considered the possibility that Satan causes physical pain and illness? What kind of spiritual help is available for you as you fight against the attack on your health?

_____

_____

_____

_____

_____

❧❦

Therefore take up the whole armor of God, that you may be able
to withstand in the evil day, and having done all, to stand.

—EPHESIANS 6:13

I am so thankful for this passage in Ephesians. I think it is one of the most powerful metaphors in the Bible. In some of the most poetic language ever written, God gives us instructions on how to win a battle with the enemy. I imagine myself girded with the truth. The truth in itself is a mighty weapon. Have you ever had misfortune because someone lied about you? Imagine the consequences when the lie is exposed and the truth is revealed. Truth empowers us. God's truth fights for us.

Wearing the gospel of peace as shoes for our feet, we can calmly march through our valleys. I like to think of this, visualizing the destruction of chaos as we firmly step through our trials. The shield of faith protects us from the fiery darts of Satan. He cannot really hurt us. Regardless of our circumstances, Christians belong to God. Nothing can take us away from Him. The helmet of salvation guarantees our place in Heaven, and it seals us with promises of God's protection.

The Word of God is the sword of the Holy Spirit, our Comforter. We can stand on the Word of God. We are promised God's comfort, even in the midst of our most frightening moments. I am so grateful for the comfort I have received in the midst of my pain. Prayer, our communication with God, not only allows us to radio our needs to God but it also provides a chance to receive messages from God. How wonderful it is when we know God has spoken to our spirit. We have directions—orders—from the highest commander.

God wants us to be shrouded in His whole armor, not just part of it. Did I find myself lacking some of this spiritual equipment? Yes. I was weak. I was not ready to win a battle, but God was ready to prepare me. Although my body was ravaged with pain and my spirit was tired, God had the answer. It was time for me to stand. It was time for me to fight. With God's mercy and grace, I would win.

Have you felt as though you are not well-equipped for your battle? How can you begin to put on the whole armor of God?

_____

_____

_____

_____

_____

❧❧

O dry bones, hear the word of the Lord!

—EZEKIEL 37:4

As I became more and more isolated from others, I depended upon my mother and my husband. I also saw a couple of close friends occasionally. I seldom left the house because of the pain. I spent most of my time in my bed, watching television. Much of the time I watched Christian programming. As I lay in bed, I knew that my muscle tissue was deteriorating. My teeth and gums were also affected because I could not brush them. If I did, I had the most violent electrocution pains. The rest of my body also deteriorated and grew flabby. I was ashamed to have my husband look at me.

Nothing could reach my aloneness. I felt frightened by my own isolation and withdrawal from others. The ministers on television seemed as though they had a message for everyone but me. How could I reach God? I had to let Him know that I wanted to be healed! Suddenly, I knew that God had answered me. I realized that I had not previously understood how much I needed Him. I now knew that I was not going to receive my healing on the coattails of someone else's faith. I was not going to receive it from listening to someone preach or through my weak prayers. If I wanted healing, I would have to meet God in His Word.

As I began to refresh myself with the Bible, something happened. My inner person, which had gone dry, began to be recharged. Had healing come? The answer had come. I realized how I needed more of God within me. The only way to get it was to study His Word. As I began to read it regularly, my inner person became alive again. Every part of my being began to strengthen. The physical pain was still with me, but now I felt the presence of God as I walked through the valley of the shadow of death. I was fed not only by the Bible but also by the messages of the ministers to whom I listened and by the music of Christian artists. My dry bones had been brought back to life by the Word of God.

Have you felt as though your inner being is withering? What biblical passages have empowered you as you walk through your valley?

_____

_____

_____

_____

_____

❦❦

Train up a child in the way that he should go,
And when he is old he will not depart from it.

—PROVERBS 22:6

I was reared in a Spirit-filled church before the word *charismatic* had been applied to denominations or worship style. The members of the Pentecostal church in which I was reared sang and clapped their hands to lively music, lifted their hands to pray, spoke in tongues, and believed in miracles. Trinity Broadcasting Network was not yet on the air. Most people had never heard of Pat Robertson. People in my church were referred to as Holy Rollers.

One of the best things about being reared this way was that I received the baptism of the Holy Spirit—I began to speak in another language when I prayed—at the age of twelve. It happened easily because I was a child and had the faith of one. Trusting God was not a complex issue. I knew He loved me, and I knew He would never leave me. Time and time again, though, I left Him. I did not understand what God's grace and mercy really were. I felt so unworthy. I had such low self-esteem that it was impossible to believe I could live up to God's standards. The fact is this: I could not. I cannot. What I did not understand was that no one can. It is God's love and the blood of Jesus that takes away our sin. We are not going to be perfect.

As I became a teenager, I learned difficult lessons about making myself vulnerable to others. I did not want to be vulnerable to God either. One thing I learned is that some individuals with evil hearts hide behind religion. These same people are the ones who judge others—especially young people—very harshly. Those who hide their sins behind religion want to point fingers at others so their own hypocrisy will not be discovered. To break away from some devastating experiences that occurred when I was a teenager, I decided to attend churches that were not charismatic or Pentecostal. On occasion, I would visit, but I did not want this type of worship to be a part of my lifestyle.

Pain and sickness, however, can cause a person to become desperate.

I knew I had to find a deeper experience in my worship. My mom invited me to go with her to a Pentecostal church my uncle pastors. It was a difficult decision. I thought about how growing up in a Pentecostal church had been so oppressive at times. It seemed that such innocent things could be labeled as sin. I did not want to be judged as I had in the past. Yet my spirit knew that something wonderful was waiting for me if I would only go. I stepped out in faith. I went to my uncle's church, and I am still going. Instead of finding judgment, I have found love. I have found people who will pray for me when I need them. I have received touches from God in ways that I could have never imagined. Although I walked a different path for many years, I always remembered the reality of God's wonderful touch.

Did you receive Christian training during your childhood? What did you experience as you were growing up that shaped or affected your faith?

_____

_____

_____

_____

_____

❧❧

He made the Pleiades and Orion; He turns the shadow
of death into morning and makes the day dark as night;
He calls for the waters of the sea and pours them
out on the face of the earth; the Lord is His name.

—Amos 5:8

My pain began to manifest itself more often. The pains were harsher and lasted longer. The episodes became more and more protracted. I questioned the potency of my faith. Was it insufficient? That was the only explanation I could provide for myself. The time had come, though, for me to admit that I did not have the answers. Answers come from God.

What seemed to me a simple physiological condition, a compressed cranial nerve, was causing debilitating pain. Surgeons had said that the simpler needle surgeries would not work because the area of nerve that was compressed was hidden. I had two options. One option was to have the nerve destroyed, meaning that my ability to feel, touch, and have other sensations would be significantly impaired.

I thought about the good days and how nice it was to feel my husband's touch. I cherished the hugs that came from my family and friends. Other complications might challenge my activities of daily living. I would feel nothing when brushing my teeth, chewing, or applying cosmetics. Many accounts of this procedure had been posted by those who had undergone it. Many people have written of their dissatisfaction, and I did not want to undergo this irreversible procedure. Knowing God is the Healer, I could not imagine destroying a major cranial nerve. How could I allow radiation to destroy what He created?

The second option was to have surgery on my brain stem. At times, I was terrified of it, and at other times, I considered the surgery as an option. Surgery also had risks, and I felt helpless to make a decision while my life was in so much turmoil. I had no answers. I began to feel as though I might be slipping back into the valley of the shadow of death.

In the deepest recesses of my thoughts and feelings, I remembered the promise God gave us for healing. I remembered that along with the universe He created me. Me. He designed my brain and the cranial nerves which stem from it. I knew that I could call on Him to provide relief and to support me in His utmost way. The God who created the universe would redesign the portion of my brain that was causing my despair. I knew He would! Lord, please pour out your mercy and healing power on me.

Have you had difficult decisions to make about your own medical treatments? What has God created that has brought blessings into your life?

_____

_____

_____

_____

_____

❃❃❃

When you walk through the fire, you shall not be burned, Nor
shall the flame scorch you.

—Isaiah 43:2

Summer school was over, and I was grateful. I thought I would regain strength during summer vacation, but my pain refused to subside. My prayer life had increased, my time in the Word had increased, and my faith had grown stronger. When my uncle prayed for me, I would receive a touch from God. It felt as though I was floating, but I was actually slowly falling to the floor. Falling to the floor or being "slain in the spirit" never hurt me or anyone around me. It gave me a reprieve from the pain. For a few moments, I would bask in the glory of God.

I asked God and myself how I could receive these blessings and then begin to have pain again once I got home. When my mom and I prayed and discussed my situation, she talked to me about trials. We talked about how successfully coming through a trial makes an individual stronger. Meanwhile, the pain on my face continued to feel like fire. The pains were so persistent that I could barely get out of bed. Regardless of my pain, God helped me to get ready for church. I only went once a week, on Sunday night. Each time, I was marvelously blessed.

When I remember this time, I think of how I learned to depend on God to bring me through the pain minute by minute. So many times, I had asked God to let me die. It was not that I did not cherish my life; I simply did not think I could bear the pain any longer. Now the reality of His presence was enough to give me hope about living through the pain. He was with me, and I knew it. I felt it.

Although I had not been thrown inside a fiery furnace, the fire raged within me. The only reprieve I got were the times at church when I received a touch from God. Otherwise, I had difficulty concentrating and coping with the pain. My eye hurt so badly that reading was difficult, yet the words from the Bible were crystal clear. All humans suffer. Christians sometimes suffer for God's sake. The bottom line was that I did not know why I was suffering. I hoped that my experience of going through the fire would help purify me, just as gold is purified through a process of fire and heat. I held to the promise that the fire would not overcome me.

Do you sometimes feel as though you can no longer cope with your illness? How does God help you cope with your most difficult moments?

_____

_____

_____

_____

_____

❦

Chapter 5

Renewed Day by Day

Therefore we do not lose heart. Even though our outward
man is perishing, yet the inward man is being renewed day by day.
For our light affliction, which is but for a moment, is working for
us a far more exceeding and eternal weight of glory, while we
do not look at things that are seen, but at the things which are
not seen. For the things which are seen are temporary,
but the things which are not seen are eternal.

—2 CORINTHIANS 4:16–18

I read the passage above several times a day, sometimes several times an hour. I needed the encouragement it speaks. I was growing extremely depressed because of the pain. I was terribly sad because my life had been stripped away. I needed someone's care almost constantly. The pains were violent. My anti-seizure medicines were once again increased, but they did not help. The pain medication seemed totally ineffective. Physically, I was perishing.

Just as this scripture promises, God renewed my inner strength and my faith each day. I thought about my pain and wondered if it could be considered light affliction. I realized that it could not compare to the pain Jesus endured when He took the stripes on His back for our healing and when He was crucified for our sins. I reminded myself that I could not measure time in the same way that God does. I thought about heaven. I longed for heaven.

I thought about the presence of God. I could not see Him, but I felt Him. I knew the Holy Spirit was with me. I felt Him, too. What had become most cherished in my life were things that could not be seen or touched. I lived for the daily blessings God sent me. Even while I suffered in my bed, I had the comforting touch of the Holy Spirit. I had my mother and friends who believed with me and prayed with me. I had assurance that God would see me through. I had the hope of an eternal life in the presence of God. That was enough to keep me from moment to moment, from day to day.

Do you ever feel like giving up? How can you stay attuned to God's willingness to comfort you while your symptoms are at their worst?

_____

_____

_____

_____

_____

❧❧

Have mercy on me, O Lord, for I am in trouble;
My eye wastes away with grief, Yes, my soul and my body!
—PSALM 31:9

Regardless of my own prayers and prayers said on my behalf, the pain would not relent. The pain in my right eye had grown worse and hurt constantly. At times, I felt consumed by grief. Yet, God was always with me on my journey through the fire. One morning my mother called to see how I was feeling before she went to run errands. I told her that things were going well and that I would be fine while she was gone.

Soon tremendous pains radiated throughout the entire right side of my head. Their intensity made it difficult to breathe and made my vision blur. I needed help. I sat up in my bed and began to talk to God. I told Him that it was becoming more difficult to hold onto His promises. "God, it is just You and me, and I am not going to play games. I am perishing here. You said that even though our outward person would perish that our inner being would be renewed. Help me. I need relief."

I reached by my bedside to pick up the phone because it was time to call for help. I looked at the phone in my hand, and I realized I could not understand how to make a phone call. I could not see the numbers on the phone or remember anyone's number. As I placed the phone back on the hook, it rang. I believed that God was sending me what I needed at that moment, but then I did not recognize the voice on the other end. The gentleman was a telemarketer with a huge corporation. He began to give me a sales pitch, but I interrupted him, asking if I could say something. He politely agreed. "I'm ill," I said. "I need prayer."

Then the gentleman asked if he could pray for me, and I agreed. What a powerful prayer came from his lips. I knew this man was not a casual believer. His knowledge of scripture was apparent, and his prayer quoted powerful scriptures. I was filled with hope as my spirit heard the Word of God. By the end of his prayer, I had the presence of mind to ask the gentlemen for his name. He gave me his name, and I wrote down his number. As the day progressed, my pain continued to lift until it seemed bearable.

Weeks later, I called the gentleman who had prayed for me. I told the operator I wanted to buy what he was selling, but I only wanted to buy it from him. I left my name and phone number, but I never received a call. I do not know if I was talking to a human or an angel that day. All I know is that God sent me exactly what I needed to survive my anguish. I received reassurance that my needs would be met and that my Lord would not allow my spirit to perish.

Have you felt as though you are perishing? How has God met your needs when you have felt totally helpless?

So the people shouted when the priests blew the trumpets.
And it happened when the people heard the sound of the
trumpet, and the people shouted with a great shout,
that the wall fell down flat.

—JOSHUA 6:20

I am so thankful that God provided timely messages for me as I continued to walk through my painful valley. One evening at church, my uncle's message was about Joshua's triumph as he and his tribe took the city of Jericho. I had learned about Jericho when I was a child, and it was one of my favorite Bible passages. I have often pondered the faith and obedience of the Israelites. They put their trust in God and did exactly as He instructed, marching around the walls of Jericho seven times, then shouting as the priests sounded their trumpets. The walls of the city fell, and Joshua and his people claimed their promise from God.

The main point in Uncle Ronnie's message, though, was that the Israelites shouted before the Jericho walls fell. Until I heard my uncle speak about this point, the timing of the Israelite's shout did not seem to be significant. I thought that the shout was simply part of God's instructions. My uncle offered more insight into Joshua's victory than I had. God wants us to obey and praise Him before our triumph is evident. The Israelites gave a mighty shout while the walls were still standing. Then God crumbled the mighty walls that kept His children from entering the land He had promised them.

When I heard Ronnie's message, I wanted to learn more about shouting before walls topple. I thought about how easy it is to thank God for something that I have not had to acquire on my own. I often fail to be thankful because I do not really appreciate blessings for which I have not asked. Now I needed something from God that required me to fight. I was gaining determination to celebrate victory while the enemy's walls still stood.

A few days after I heard the message about Jericho, I was preparing to visit my friend Susie while she was in the hospital. When I began to groom myself, terrible electrocution pains struck my mouth and face. At first, I felt concerned that the pain would stop me from going to see Susie. Not only did I have to finish grooming myself but I also had to drive to another city to see her. I remembered Joshua's army, and I still desired their powerful faith. I closed my eyes, and I thanked God for bringing down the enemy's walls. I visualized them as they fell, and I continued to praise God. The pain left immediately.

My mother rode along with me to visit Susie. We had the opportunity to pray for Susie while she was in pain. By learning how to shout before the walls came down, I became a source of encouragement that afternoon. Thank you, Lord, for helping me to shout "Victory!" before my walls actually fell.

Have you ever felt as though there were walls in your life that prevented you from winning your battles? How can you bring down the walls that stand in the way of God's blessings?

_____

_____

_____

_____

_____

❧❧

Confess your trespasses to one another, and pray for
one another, that you may be healed. The effective, fervent
prayer of a righteous man avails much.

—JAMES 5:16

I will never know how many people prayed for me during this time, but am thankful for those that did. How blessed I am to have people join together to pray for me, sometimes for hours on end. Throughout the summer, prayers came through telephone calls, visits, and during church services. Just as the summer semester ended, a breakthrough came. The pain had reduced, but I was still quite weak.

Fall semester began, and I missed the first night of class. I was still very weak from the pain and could not have endured a commute. That was not the real reason I missed class, though. I was actually so confused that I thought class was on Tuesday night rather than Monday night. I was shocked when Stephanie called to see where I was. I realized that I had not been ready to go back yet, and during prayer, God assured me that I had forgotten because I was not strong enough to go yet.

When I returned to school, I sought counseling. I had been depressed for several months. The pace of school as well as the pain itself had caused tremendous stress. Socially, I felt as though I was back at square one because I once again felt uneasy meeting new people. Although a few classmates from the previous class remained, most of the people in my classes were new. For the first time, I found myself really just wanting to be at home.

I continued to go to counseling. It helped me deal with my anxiety about school, and I grew from this experience. As the semester continued, my pain grew worse. Concentrating was very difficult. I wondered if school was the right place for me. I could not imagine giving up. I remembered my prayer during summer break. I had asked God to help me do His work, whatever that happened to be. My spirit had quickened, and I knew God wanted me to proceed to work for Him. I continued my studies, and God brought me through every assignment, every test, one step at a time.

How has God answered one of your prayers? How do we benefit when we pray for others?

_____

_____

_____

_____

_____

❧❧

I will bring the blind by a way they did not know;
I will lead them in paths they have not known. I will make
darkness light before them, And crooked places straight. These
things I will do for them, And not forsake them.

—ISAIAH 42:16

Recently as I stood near the altar at church, I had one of the most important realizations of my life—a true epiphany. I had been experiencing tremendous physical pain as well as emotional turmoil that involved family members whom I have not mentioned. In my prayers, God had comforted me. Yet the pain was sharp and deep. Ronnie placed his hand on my shoulder and said, "Kathy, you are not here by accident. God has a plan for your life." Most of us have heard before that God has a plan for our lives. I have heard it many, many times. When my Uncle Ronnie said this, I struggled with the idea so much that all I could do was look down at the floor. It seemed that plans for my life were once again being destroyed by trigeminal neuralgia.

As I stared at the floor, tears came to my eyes. Ronnie repeated the phrase. While I looked at the floor, I realized that I was standing on the very foundation of the building in which my mother and father had met. Their marriage only lasted a few weeks and was over before my mother's pregnancy was discovered. My mother was young, and rearing a child on her own proved to be very difficult. Most of my life, I felt like an impediment, an accident, but suddenly I realized that God planned my birth.

I looked up from the floor and lifted my eyes toward heaven. Then I began to experience God in a way I had never known before. My feet and the platform heels I wore seemed to grow wings. With my eyes closed and without music, I danced before the Lord. I celebrated my birth and thanked God for putting me here. I thanked God for allowing His Spirit to rest on me.

I thanked Him for my Granny's persistence. When she moved back to Green Cove Springs, the church had been closed, padlocked. Granny was instrumental in getting the church reopened, not knowing that one day her youngest son would be its pastor. She never knew it would become her oldest grandchild's true home. I thank God I have something on earth to call my true home. In spite of all the moving around I have done, this church has remained constant. Many of my relatives have married there; others have had their funerals there. Like many others in my family, I was dedicated to God in this church when I was just a baby. For me, this little church in Green Cove Springs has become holy ground.

Have you questioned your own value? How does God help us follow His plan for our lives?

_____

_____

_____

_____

_____

The Lord will fight for you, and you shall hold your peace.

—Exodus 14:14

As my determination to pursue a closer walk with God grew, the pain became more violent. When God's anointing touched me, the pain would begin to rage within my face and head. Sometimes it occurred when my uncle prayed for me, and at other times, it would happen when my mother prayed. It even occurred as I basked in God's spirit or when I prayed alone.

To have the fire of pain storm within my face as I experience God's touch has been difficult for me to understand. I have struggled with the thought of how this can occur when I feel God's Spirit so strongly. I have tried to look at the situation objectively. If it were happening to someone else, I would tell him or her that it is spiritual warfare manifested in the body. Yet it was hard for me to accept this. Who am I that the enemy would fight so hard to prevent me from being pain-free? I am not Job. I am not a minister or a church musician. Many times I have asked myself why the enemy would not move on, to wage war against someone else. Physically and emotionally exhausted, I have wondered how I could continue to fight the enemy.

Just as each of us is important to God, we are also significant challengers of Satan. Every time we read and speak God's Word, we are fortified by God's Spirit. God's Spirit dwells in us, and the enemy will do whatever he can to stop our spiritual progress. One method he uses is an attempt to steal the peace that God gives us. Our peace, which prevails even in the most difficult of life's circumstances, is something that the world notices. It impresses people who are not Christians. It inspires those with whom we have regular contact.

Because my relationship with God began to grow, the enemy attempted to target me. It had nothing to do with who I am or who I am not. Because I am a child of God, the enemy could not win. I am clothed in God's armor, and through prayer I resisted defeat. When the pain rose up as someone prayed for me, I would also rise. If kneeling, I stood. If standing, I raised my hands to the Lord. If in a car, I used the opportunity to plead the blood of Jesus. The more we fight the fight of faith, the stronger we become. I thank God for spiritual strength. Although the battle was not over, it was already won!

Have you wondered if you can continue to endure your illness?
How can we join God's army of peace?

_____

_____

_____

_____

_____

❧❧

If we love one another, God abides in us, and
His love has been perfected in us.

—1 JOHN 4:12

One of the best things about returning to the church where my grand-parents and other relatives attended is that I have the opportunity to worship with people whom I have known since my childhood. Although the church has grown quite a bit, it is still full of familiar faces. This is especially comforting to me because I have relocated so many times. Throughout my life, I have been blessed by true friends. Distance has dissolved many of these friendships, and I have often felt lonely because my friends were far away.

The isolation that resulted from my illness was devastating. God provided me with relief so that I could attend church functions. Many of the activities were also attended by my aunts, uncles, and cousins. During church activities, family reunions, and other celebrations, I had to use earplugs made to reduce the noise on airplane flights. The earplugs actually helped quite a bit. The only drawback is that I often cannot understand what is being said by the individual with whom I am talking. It is not unusual that he or she does not know about the earplugs, so communication becomes difficult. Afterwards, I would ask myself why I bothered going to the event.

So many times I went to church when the pain was so intense that it prevented me from talking. I have learned, however, that I did not have to say a word. Friends and family at church could look into my eyes and understand that I was in pain. Sometimes I was embraced by women from church I barely know, and I saw love and compassion in their eyes. I was comforted by their acceptance. I thank God not only for the love we have for each other but also for the method that people use to communicate through body language. It often surpasses any message that can be expressed through words.

Something wonderful happens when Christians take each other's hands. Even in silence, two Christians can agree. Agreement puts power

75

in our prayers. In Matthew 18:19, Jesus tells us that if two of us agree in prayer, that our heavenly Father will answer. I am so glad that love is a language all its own. It has the power to accept others in spite of their shortcomings and weaknesses. Love gives us the ability to reach out to others when we might feel as though we have nothing to give. I thank God for the love that abides in His people. I am grateful that I have friends—old and new—at my church.

Has God blessed you with a good friend? How can you show God's love to other people?

_____

_____

_____

_____

_____

❧❦

And whatever you ask in My name, that I will do,
that the Father may be glorified in the Son. If you ask
anything in My name, I will do it.

—JOHN 14:13–14

I believe that God's Word is infallible. I might not always fully comprehend the meaning of a scripture, but my faith in God allows me to accept it. Faith is a powerful and beautiful gift from God. It provides hope and helps us remain steadfast and calm. I thank God for the many prayers that He has answered, requests made in the name of Jesus.

Sometimes I wondered why my pain continued to return. I questioned the strength of my own faith. Once I had sincerely believed that the trigeminal neuralgia was gone, I began to have a lifestyle like a person without a disability or illness. When the pain returned, I wondered if God had been displeased with me. Because I wanted to please God, I began to surrender more and more of my life to Him. My relationship with my Savior had grown much stronger. God had become foremost in my life when I began to love Him with my whole heart. In the name of Jesus, I asked for my healing to return. I had asked for the pain to leave.

I received marvelous blessings when the anointing flowed throughout the church congregation. I could not understand why the pain often intensified at this point. Although I had not received my healing, God answered other prayers. I believed that God would receive glory through my healing, not my illness. Had I proved to God that I loved and believed in Jesus? I asked God to help me understand my predicament. I wanted to know why I had not received my healing yet. I wanted to know what I was doing wrong.

Along the way, God began to reveal some things to me about healing. Further confirmation came that I was indeed wrestling with the enemy. Sometimes the electrocution pain spread throughout the right side of my body. My right arm and leg shook, and standing or walking was almost impossible. Then I would begin to choke and to feel as though I could not breathe.

My mother saw this happen one day. She jumped out of the car and came to my side. With boldness from God, she rebuked Satan in the name of Jesus. The pain left, the choking stopped, and I could breathe. Later that evening, the same thing happened in church. My uncle stopped the service, and I went forward for prayer. Immediately, I was fine. Satan had been stopped by the name of Jesus. God took me though my valley one day at time, one moment at a time. I needed to learn what trusting in Him really meant. I was also learning that sometimes healing is a process, not an instantaneous event. Lord, thank You for being with me every step of the way. I will continue to trust in You.

Have you ever wondered why you have not received your healing? What prayer has God answered for you?

_____

_____

_____

_____

_____

❧❧

No Fear in Love

There is no fear in love; but perfect love
casts out fear, because fear involves torment. But he who
fears has not been made perfect in love.

—1 JOHN 4:18

The pain began to strike every time I walked out the church door. I felt as though I were being taunted by the enemy. Fear crept in. So did embarrassment. How often would I have need for special prayer? I was afraid people would look at me in a negative manner, but I could not let my fear or embarrassment stop me. My only hope was to continue to present my plight to God, whether alone in my home or at the front of the church.

During this time, I decided that it did not matter what others thought. I also realized that my sisters and brothers in the Lord have their own battles. Judging others is not a priority for them. Praying for others is.

One night at church, I had received a mighty touch from God. I knew He was paying attention to me. The pain had left, and I felt relief in my body, my spirit, and my emotions. Church dismissed, and I picked up my purse. I was just a few steps away from my Aunt Brenda, and I began to talk to her. The moment I did, pain raced through my facial nerves and muscles, freezing them and my ability to talk. I began to cry.

Brenda and my mother began to pray with me. Brenda mentioned fear in her prayer. I had not mentioned my fear to anyone, but she sensed it. It is another one of the enemy's tools. Fear drives a wedge between an individual and God. It speaks loudly and asks God if His mercy can sustain us. Fear says that we are not sure. In 2 Corinthians 12:9, Jesus tells us that His grace is sufficient for us and that His strength is made perfect through our weaknesses. Through this promise, we can find assurance that God is going to take care of us. We can depend on His perfect strength. Our weaknesses are opportunities for God to bestow His love and power in our lives.

In His Word, God does not tell us that we will not have pain and suffering. He tells us to expect it. He wants to be our shelter. The Holy Spirit wants to comfort us. Our anxieties, fears, and doubts are opportunities for God to reveal Himself to us. If we admit these insecurities to God, He will help us cope with them. Negative thoughts and feelings can be difficult to extinguish, but I learned that open and consistent communication with God helps me. God never promised that we would go through life without tribulations. What He promised was a way to eliminate our torment through His perfect love.

Have you had moments when your illness caused you to be frightened? How has God helped you through a fear-provoking experience?

_____

_____

_____

_____

_____

❦

But many who are first will be last, and the last first.

—MARK 10:31

The words of Jesus in this scripture have always baffled me. I have heard several ministers speak about their own interpretations and how difficult it was to arrive at an understanding of the verse. I do not pretend to know what it means, but I do know that something spectacular happened that makes me think of this scripture. In theory, if the first person becomes the last person, then two people have traded places. One of my most glorious experiences is about trading places.

One night when I was in church, our congregation was blessed with a mighty demonstration of the Holy Spirit's presence. I could feel God with every fiber of my being. The congregation was standing, praising God. My mother stood to the left of me, and her husband John was to her left. To my right, Kay Crenshaw stood. Kay's husband was to her right. I was sandwiched between my mother and the Crenshaws, with whom I was barely acquainted. My uncle was standing in the aisle, speaking to the congregation.

I felt a stillness that penetrated me as I worshipped. Then quickly, my arms began to jerk. I felt like a marionette whose strings were controlled by a powerful hand. Other parts of my body began to jerk. Then I felt something like a great wind around me. It seemed to pick me up and toss me into the pew. I rested in the pew but a moment, my body still jerking. Still having no control over my body, I jumped up from the pew and stood again in my place. In a moment, the jerking subsided. I opened my eyes. I was sitting next to Kay's husband, and she was sitting next to my mother.

People around us were smiling and shaking their heads in disbelief. I could hear my uncle laughing. "Now folks, that is the way things used to be," he said. I was now standing next to a man I barely knew, wondering what was going to happen next. After a couple of minutes, Kay and I went back to our original seats. This time, we were in control of our own movements. I have wished many times that I could have seen this as the

81

others around us saw it. People said that Kay and I crisscrossed each other. We were both tossed into each others' seats in the pew.

Even though I did not see any of it, I remember how it felt. It was as though a rushing mighty wind, like the one described in Acts, had touched me with its power. My spirit was quickened in a way I could have never imagined. The next few days were filled with a "high" that could come only from God. I thank God that He reached down to bless me in a truly unique way.

Have your priorities been rearranged because of your illness? How can your relationship with God become or continue to be your main concern?

_____

_____

_____

_____

_____

❧❀❧

Our bodies had no rest, but we were troubled on every side.
Outside were conflicts, inside were fears.

—2 Corinthians 7:5

As I reached the end of the semester, I felt very dissatisfied with my responsibilities. To maintain my part-time studies, I had to make them my first priority. In one of my classes, I had a test every other Monday. The tests covered medical information, something new for me. I studied a great deal of the time so that I could understand and memorize the information. Because tests were on Mondays, I spent many of my days, including Sundays, preoccupied with medical information rather than with spiritual edification.

My family gave me tremendous support as I continued in school. My mother helped with meals. My husband did most of the laundry and plenty of other household chores. My husband's brother and his wife offered me the opportunity to spend Monday nights in their home so I would not have to drive back home late at night. In spite of everyone's efforts to keep my load light, I had been ill most of the semester. Besides pain from trigeminal neuralgia, I also had allergy attacks and colds. My stomach was upset from medications. I realized that I was in the same situation I had been in years before when I had resigned from my teaching position.

I talked to God regularly about my situation. It provided me with great relief just to tell Him that I wanted to spend more time with Him. He knew my heart, and He continued to bless me every time I went to church. I received blessings from Him at home, too. At least six weeks between the fall and spring semester would belong to me, and I could give them to God. I was encouraged. I believed this was enough time to garner physical and spiritual strength. I would take only one class in the spring semester. I knew I had to slow my pace.

Just a few days after the break began, I had another allergy attack. It was followed by a cold. I developed laryngitis, and I coughed relentlessly. The coughing resulted in severe trigeminal pain. I began to experience electrocution-type pains throughout every day. I had grown more tired during break than I had been at the end of the semester. I continued to pray about school. I was almost finished with my master's degree, needing only two more classes and an internship. I wanted to finish. I believed that God would revive me so that I could minister to individuals with illnesses and disabilities.

I prayed that God's will, not mine, would be accomplished in my life. I began to relinquish my own idea of what God wanted me to do. I asked Him to deliver me from my suffering. I promised that I would keep Him at the center of my life. The conflicts and the fears began to disappear. The break had not physically revived me, but my spirit had been fed. God continued to eliminate the conflicts and fears that I had allowed to concern me.

Have you been able to find rest? How can God help you resolve conflicts in your life?

_____

_____

_____

_____

_____

❦

Testify in the Lord, that you should no longer walk
as the rest of the Gentiles walk, in the futility of their mind.
—EPHESIANS 4:17

At the beginning of January, I received another blessing. Class would start two weeks later than scheduled. I thanked God for the extra time to recuperate and to spend with Him. The extra time was certainly an answer to my prayer. The delay in the schedule also gave me the opportunity to spend time with my friend Mary, who was preparing to move out of state. In many ways, Mary has been a mentor to me. Her prayers for me have been consistent, even before I became ill.

One evening Mary and I decided to go out to dinner. I read to her a letter I had written about God's love. It testified of God's faithfulness, and how He brought me back to a Pentecostal church to witness the mighty works of the Holy Spirit. It spoke of emotional healing, something I had not asked for but had received. God had healed my hurt from issues that resulted from past experiences that occurred as I attended church. Mary encouraged me, as she had many times before, to write about my experiences as I pursued God's healing. I held in my hand the only piece I had written. As we talked about my healing, something in my spirit quickened. I knew what to do. I told Mary that I would write about my experience, but that I could not do it unless I gave others the opportunity to concurrently tell their own stories.

I began to ask God how I should do this. I wanted to let others know that He walks with us as we suffer. He understands our pain. His son Jesus experienced it in a way that I will never be able to comprehend. I began to write *With Great Mercy*, and God was with me as I typed every word. I had no outline, only guidance from the Lord. I felt His presence, and He blessed me tremendously as I began to write testimony of His mercy, faithfulness, and grace.

As I began writing, I felt the assurance that I was doing God's will. So many times in life, I have been determined to do my own. I thank God that He gave me the willingness to listen to Him and to obey Him. God spoke to me through Mary, and my desire is to speak to others about His promises to keep us even in our darkest hours.

Do you have experiences that testify of God's love? How can you help others to find encouragement through Jesus Christ?

_____

_____

_____

_____

_____

❧❧

Yes, and all who desire to live godly in Christ Jesus
will suffer persecution.
—2 TIMOTHY 3:12

*W*hen I had written just a few entries, I had a terribly frightening experience while I was alone. My husband and I were adding a breakfast room to our home. Our superintendent was normally at our home during workdays. This young man had left for a few minutes to exchange an item at a nearby store. I was sitting in our study, working on an entry for this devotional. I had just typed "The Lord is our Healer."

Suddenly, one of the worst pains I have ever endured struck the corner of my lip and penetrated my face, spreading throughout my nose, eye, ear, and jaw. The pain struck quickly and violently, as though someone had applied direct blows to my face. I realized that the force of the pain had knocked me out of my chair. I regained my balance and stood upright. The pains continued to come. I lay down on the floor and cried out to God, pleading the blood of Jesus.

The harshest of the pains subsided, leaving me extremely weak. I reached up for the phone and put it down on the floor. Immediately, I called Mary and she began to pray for me. After prayer, we continued to talk. Soon I heard our superintendent come in. I left Mary on the phone while I told him what had happened. Then I assured Mary that I would not be alone and that my pain had diminished.

Before I went to my bedroom to lie down, I looked at my computer screen as I saved my work. The Lord is our Healer. Through God's mercy, we are healed. This is the message I hope to convey. I want others to know that living for God results in joy regardless of our circumstances. All a person has to do is want God's love more than anything else, and He will be faithful to us.

I realized the enemy did not want me to write about my experience. Satan was attempting to squelch my testimony. I did not understand this because I am not a person the world considers important. I do not have fame or riches. I hold no titles. It seemed odd that the enemy would be so intent on preventing the writing of a devotional. Then I remembered my desire to live a godly life in Christ Jesus, and I knew my horrible pain was really about my relationship with Him. The enemy wanted me to become angry with God, to relinquish hope. I refused to let go of God's love. I have spent most of my life outside His will. Now that I had learned how to walk with God day by day, not even the worst of pain could stop me from serving God. I have His mercy, and it is sufficient for all things.

Do you want to live a godly life? How can God's mercy help during persecution?

_____

_____

_____

_____

_____

꽃꽃

My bones are pierced in me at night,
And my gnawing pains take no rest.

—JOB 30:17

Pains continued as the night came. The next morning, I was still in bed. My mother planned to come over as soon as she finished her exercise class. Our superintendent left to run a quick errand. As I lay in bed, I was attacked with the most severe pain I had experienced. It permeated my right cheek and jaw. I experienced an identical pain in the same location, every two to three seconds. My body could not stay still, and I moved uncontrollably on the bed. I rose to my knees and faced my headboard. I held onto the top of it as the pains continued. I heard my little dog run around my house barking, trying to get help for me. I could not speak, but I could scream. Everything in and around my mouth was frozen, yet the pain was so harsh that I could not stop screaming.

As I stood on my knees, my desperation to stop the pain was my only thought. I could not speak. I could not pray. My eyes were closed, and I faced my wall. As the pain continued, I began to think of the stripes that Jesus Christ took on His back so that we would be healed. I was humbled by my own frailty. I could not even bear my own pain. I could not imagine offering myself as a sacrifice to help others. How marvelous is Jesus Christ who endured a cruel beating while His tormentors mocked Him. He endured the beating for me, so that I could be healed.

As quickly as the intense electrocution pains came, they subsided. Because I was frightened and weak, I called someone to sit with me. Electrocution pains of less intensity continued throughout the night and then again the next day. I sought God as I never had before. I loved Him more than ever. I had gained more determination to live for Him. The enemy's plan to defeat me with pain was useless because the blood of Jesus covers me. I belong to God, and He is my protector.

I thank God for providing people to pray for me. My mother refused to leave me alone. We prayed throughout the morning. My mother talked to my Uncle Ronnie. Our church was completing a new sanctuary, and the congregation was at the church to do some landscaping. They took a break from their work to pray just for me. My spirit knew when the prayers of the congregation began. Relief came to my body. Joy flooded the room. I was able to function the rest of the day.

Have you experienced unrelenting pain? How can our own suffering bring us closer to God?

_____

_____

_____

_____

_____

❧❧

Therefore gird up the loins of your mind, be sober,
and rest your hope fully upon the grace that is to be brought
to you at the revelation of Jesus Christ.

—1 PETER 1:13

ains returned in the night. I was in the midst of the fiercest battle I had ever encountered. The pain radiated throughout the right side of my head and face. My body was so weak that I could barely stand up. Concentrating was impossible. My faith, which had recently soared, was shaken.

I had a tremendous desire to go to church that morning because it was the last morning service in our old sanctuary, the building that holds such a precious place in my heart. My mother had also wanted to go, but she came over to pray with me instead. Hours of prayer passed. My mother read the Bible to me. We asked God to relieve the pain and to give me the ability to brush my teeth so I could go to church that night. The pain remained as forceful as ever.

I got up from my bed in spite of it. I walked into the study and began to listen to Christian music that I have stored on my computer. It helped me worship, and I began to feel hope. It was as though the message in the music had renewed my spirit. I listened to several songs and walked back into my bedroom. Once again, I asked God to help me brush my teeth. This simple everyday act can create the worst symptoms of all. Often when I tried to brush, I had to hold onto the sink because my body began to faint.

I got my toothbrush ready and began to brush. I experienced some pain, but it was minimal compared to what I sometimes endured. I was able to thoroughly brush my teeth. I knew that God had helped me and that He was making provisions for me to attend church. I got dressed and went to church. What a special night it was, not only because it was the last night in that little building but also because I received a special touch from the Lord. The people who had prayed for me expressed their happiness to see me. God's love is so huge, so marvelous. As the night progressed, I was able to concentrate again. I could participate in a conversation. God was preparing me for changes that would soon take place in my life.

Has concentration been difficult during your illness? How can you focus more thoroughly on God's love and healing power?

_____

_____

_____

_____

_____

❧❧

> I will stand my watch And set myself on the rampart,
> And watch to see what He will say to me, And what I will
> answer when I am corrected.
>
> —HABAKKUK 2:1

I was terrified of being alone. I was afraid that the enemy would strike again with the torturous pain if I were by myself. My mother took me home with her. In fact, she and I slept in the same room so that she could pray for me when the pains awakened me. I stayed with her a week. During that time, she cooked for my husband, and prepared food for me that did not have to be chewed. When my mother had to run errands, Mary volunteered to be with me.

We were in the heart of warfare. I had only two options. I could blame God for my suffering, but blame was not in my heart. I was assured that He had not caused the pain, and I did not want the bitterness that attaches itself to blame. The only other thing I could do was to hold fast. I was ready to hear from God. I had so many questions. What did He want from me? Was my life so displeasing to Him that He would allow the pain to torment me indefinitely? Did God want me to give up something? Was sin or bitterness in my heart?

For a week, we held a vigil on my behalf. One day our friend Cherry spent the day praying with my mother and me. My physical strength waned, but I was encouraged by the love of family and friends. Although I had people who would ensure I was not alone, I had to find a way to regain spiritual strength. I thought about the suffering of Jesus and about His aloneness during the time of physical torture. I continued to love Him even more for willingly presenting Himself as a sacrifice for my sins. Through prayer, I was impressed to keep on. I did not receive a reprimand from God. He did not reveal to me that I should give up something.

I felt unsure about asking God to examine my heart. Although introspection is a difficult process, I gained strength from it. If I could place myself before God in this manner, surely I could stand up to the enemy. I had the whole armor of God. I had the blood of Jesus. I began to feel stronger in the Lord. My drive to write about God's love and faithfulness began to increase. Even on my worst of days, God revealed to me what I should read from His Word and how I could relate it to my experience. Thank you, Lord, for the family and friends who stood watch over me.

Have you needed someone to stand watch for your benefit? What might God ask you to do, even on your worst of days?

_____

_____

_____

_____

_____

꧁꧂

Then Jesus said to His disciples, "If anyone desires to
come after Me, let him deny himself, and take up
his cross, and follow Me."

—MATTHEW 16:24

During the vigil, my first class of the semester met. At this point,
school was not a priority. Survival was. Because I was very close
to finishing my master's degree, the thought of quitting my studies sad-
dened me. I contacted the university, but I did not appeal to them to
excuse me from classes. I did not know that I would be able to complete
the course even if given the opportunity to complete it at my own pace.
I prayed that God's plan would prevail. I was ready to accept leniency
from the university, but I was also prepared to withdraw.

Speaking was very difficult, and Mary came over to help me. She took
me to my own home so that I could gather the documentation necessary for the university to understand my medical situation. Mary called
the university for me. Forms arrived via my facsimile machine, and we
completed them. The wheels were in motion, and soon I would know
my status as a student. When Mary and I finished, I was exhausted and
felt totally devoured by the pain, uncertainty, and stress.

Letting go of the master's degree was difficult. I did not want to give
up. I could hear these words racing through my mind: "I am not a quitter. I am not a quitter." I remembered so many times that I had worked
diligently in spite of my pain. I thought of the people who had helped
me with transportation. Quitting now would be a difficult decision for
me to reconcile. Mary took me back to my mother's, and I rested and
meditated upon God's Word. I thought about my recent experiences
with the Holy Spirit. I remembered that during prayer, God had strongly
impressed me to accomplish His work. Now it looked as though that
opportunity might vanish.

The next day, a university official told me that perhaps it would be
best if I withdrew. For an instant, I thought my heart would break. Then
a sense of peace swept through my mental and spiritual being. I was free.

I could pray as much as I wanted. I could go to church as much as I was able. I would begin to have adequate rest.

I thought about my desire to provide help and assurance to individuals who are coping with illnesses. How could this desire be in conflict with God's plan for my life? I began to realize that God's plan and my plan might not be the same. As I prayed about it, my understanding grew. I had confirmation that God wanted me to use my experiences to help others. God insisted on being a part of it. If I were to write about my illness and how I became a stronger Christian because of it, God's mercy would be the message. The time had come to do things God's way, not mine. It was a matter of following His will.

Have you been struggling with letting something go? How do you follow Jesus in your daily walk?

_____

_____

_____

_____

_____

❦❦

But you must continue in the things which you have learned
and been assured of, knowing from whom you have learned them.
—2 TIMOTHY 3:14

God faithfully confirmed His will. Sometimes I would awaken with the name of a book of the Bible on my lips. As I read through the passages, I would feel God's anointing as I read a particular verse. Sometimes I knew exactly how the verse would help me tell my story. At other times, I had to ask God how the verse was relevant. He always helped me. The process was not stressful or laborious. Every time I wrote about how God helped me cope with the pain, my spirit grew stronger. Yet the pain refused to subside.

When I attended church services, my uncle or a guest minister often referred to a passage to which God had directed me just a day or two earlier. Often the speaker mentioned the verse and then explained that he had not intended to use it in the message. Time after time, the speaker explained that as he spoke, he felt God leading him to this scripture. I knew that God was blessing the congregation with His Word, and I also realized that He was providing confirmation for me.

I needed the confirmation and reassurance because the pain continued to rage. My speech had once again grown difficult to understand. Every morning, I was awakened by severe pain. I would not get up from bed unless I took time to pray earnestly for relief. I thank God that I had no pressure from my studies. I had the time to pray for God's mercy. I had the time to rest in His love. I had time to praise Him for the healing He promises in His word. Through prayer, I gained the strength to cope with the pain. I continued writing. Oh, how I longed to be well!

Although pain kept me at home, God continued to reassure me. I began to share entries from *With Great Mercy* with others. Although I was in the midst of a tremendous valley, God provided a way for me to write something that could bless others. Once again, I was stepping into a role that allowed me to help others. God was answering my prayers.

I thought about how my life might look to others. I had difficulty speaking. Sometimes my own mother could not understand me. I had electrocution pains on a regular basis. They increased if I stepped out into the winter wind. My right eye hurt constantly. There was no evidence that my health would improve, but I had gained mighty faith. God had given me the opportunity to trust Him, and my spirit was continually renewed.

Have you asked yourself how you can continue to have faith? How can you find God's assurance?

_____

_____

_____

_____

_____

❧❧

For she said, "If only I may touch His clothes,
I shall be made well."

—MARK 5:28

One evening when I arrived at church, I began to think about the Bible's account of the woman who had been ill for twelve years. This woman was healed when she reached out for the hem of Jesus' garment. Her touch was so full of faith that Jesus turned His attention to her. Jesus spoke to her, telling her that her faith had made her well.

I was determined to touch Jesus with my faith. Early in the service, the congregation prayed. I told God about my desire to touch Jesus. I will touch Jesus. I will reach out to Him until I touch Him. I know that trigeminal neuralgia can go into spontaneous remission. If this can happen to people who do not ask God for healing, surely God would provide total healing for me.

All during the evening, the woman who had the "issue of blood" stayed on my mind. Although my uncle was preaching on a different subject, he began to discuss her healing. Uncle Ronnie told the congregation that he was getting away from his prepared subject but felt the Lord leading him to mention this woman. The Holy Spirit had moved both our minds in this direction. I knew that tonight something special would happen.

I prayed earnestly at the altar as the service drew to a close. My uncle and my mother prayed with me. The pain raged in my face as we prayed, but I had learned that it was a trick of the enemy. Satan wanted to plant disbelief, but he could not. I stood before the Lord proclaiming my faith. I felt God's presence. I knew that my faith had touched Him.

By the end of the service, something had changed. I walked out into the cold night air with my scarf draped around my neck. As I had entered the church before the service, I had a scarf and a windbreaker wrapped around my head to protect me from the cold. Even a second of cold air would have provoked violent pains before the service began. After church was dismissed, the air was colder, but I did not need my scarf.

God had heard my prayers. I thanked Him again for confirming my healing. Through His love, I would continue toward His healing virtue.

Have you ever felt desperate to gain the attention of Jesus? What have you experienced that proves God hears your prayers?

_____

_____

_____

_____

_____

❧❦

For His anger is but for a moment, His favor is for life; Weeping
may endure for a night, But joy comes in the morning.

—PSALM 30:5

So many times during the course of my illness, I felt that I had
incurred God's wrath. The more time I spent in prayer and in His
word, however, the more I realized that suffering and trials are a part of
life. Humans cannot escape them. Life sometimes breaks people's hearts.
People hurt. My situation was not an exception.

Pain and agony causes depression. I had learned its cycle. When the
terrible pains began, I felt hopeless. I did not know how to cope, and my
losses were magnified because I was held captive. I could not escape the
pain or my bed. Exhaustion from pain and lack of sleep further contributed to feelings of hopelessness. After the pain would go into remission,
the depression would lift. I would begin to function again. If I had been
down for an extended period, then it would be necessary to readjust
from isolation into social situations again.

What some individuals never understood is that my pain, loss, and
isolation caused the depression. My efforts to earn a degree contributed
to my exhaustion, and the depression was a result of my situation. I did
not get sick because I was depressed. How frustrated I felt when a person who barely knew me made a snap judgment about the relationship
between depression and my illness. Sometimes this conclusion has been
made by individuals who should have known better, but medical and
rehabilitation professionals are not always informed about the psycho-
logical component that accompanies trigeminal neuralgia.

God knows everything. He understands the physical and emotional
turmoil evoked by pain. Jesus Christ suffered in His death in ways that
I cannot imagine. He knows firsthand the reality of pain, and He provides us with coping methods. God's presence quickens our spirit, and
the Holy Spirit provides us with His comfort. God knows when we have
endured all we can, and He will not allow us to break. We must hold our
hearts out to Him for protection.

God began to lift my depression even while I was in the midst of severe pain. I did not ask Him to do it. It happened naturally as I continued in my efforts to touch Jesus. How much easier it is to remain passive and ask Jesus to touch us. Yet we impress God more when we reach out for Him. I began to have joy even while enduring the worst of the pain. Joy of the Lord transcends circumstances and pain. Joy gives us a testimony. Joy came to me as I allowed myself to trust more thoroughly in God.

Have you felt sad or depressed with your illness? How can God help you overcome these feelings?

_____

_____

_____

_____

_____

✖✖

Who Himself [Jesus] bore our sins in His own
body on the tree, that we, having died to sins, might live for
righteousness—by whose stripes you were healed.

—1 PETER 2:24

Facts, as well as joy, transcend circumstances. God lovingly gave me joy in spite of my physical pain. Jesus endured a merciless beating to provide healing for us. We might be sick or in pain, yet the fact remains that by His stripes, we *were* healed. God's Word does not lie. It tells us that Jesus bore our sins so we would have an opportunity to live for righteousness.

For me, living for righteousness is not a chore. It is a privilege. Seeking God's love and healing power brings me closer to Him. As I have drawn closer to God, two things have happened. I have begun to better understand righteousness. I have been influenced by the Holy Spirit as I have walked more closely with God. God's own righteousness has transformed me, and I have begun to want more of God's Spirit. I feel His peace and I want to be more like Him.

I thank God for the opportunity to know Him in a more intimate way. During the healing process, my faith was consistently boosted. My security level increased, and assurance of an ability to function normally grew stronger. The fear of pain became distant. I experienced God's victories in my battles with the enemy. I did not change by accident. I have changed because I decided to believe in His Word rather than to look at my circumstances.

God heals not only our physical pain but also our hearts. We can walk in faith by clinging to God's promises. Jesus bore our agony. Although we cannot escape sorrow in this lifetime, we have the assurance that it is temporary. If the circumstances that create our turmoil do not change, God gives us peace by renewing our hearts. He gives us joy in spite of painful situations.

It does not matter what the root of our pain is. It could be emotional, mental, social, or physical. God's mercy provides us with the ability to walk through the fire without harming our spirits. We cannot see Him, but we can feel Him if we are willing to get close. Lord, thank You for showing me how to look at Your truths rather than my own circumstances.

Have your circumstances ever seemed to cloud the reality of Jesus' love? How can you gain more hope through the sacrifice of God's Son?

_____

_____

_____

_____

_____

�֍❧

The Lord shall judge the peoples; Judge me, O Lord, according to my righteousness, And according to my integrity within me.
—PSALM 7:8

Sometimes stressful events threaten joy. One of the most difficult things I have done is to file a claim for social security disability benefits. It was a two-year process. No one in the social security system has been disrespectful or unkind to me. It has been the nature of the application process that has created tension.

Immediately after I began my last teaching job, some individuals were in the teachers' workroom selling insurance policies. The sales representatives approached me about a disability policy. I had just met Page. She was ill and was younger than I. I watched her come to work in pain, day after day. I realized that illness can happen to anyone, so I decided that I would buy a policy. I thank God for giving me the wisdom to do it.

My insurance company requires its policyholders to apply for Social Security benefits. I did not want to do it. I began to go through the motions, believing that I would be able to return to work before the process would culminate in a hearing. I never considered the possibility that when my hearing actually occurred that I would consider myself a valid candidate for benefits.

I had prayed that God would give me a kind judge. I also prayed for favor with the judge. I told God that I would trust Him with the decision. I did not want a difficult day in court. My illness was not something I wanted to talk about. I had been walking in faith, believing that I would get better. Now I had to discuss the details of my illness with someone I had never met.

One prayer had been answered before I walked into the hearing. My attorney had told me that my judge was a pleasant and courteous individual. In spite of this knowledge, I was incredibly nervous. I had awakened in the middle of the night in severe pain and was physically and emotionally depleted for the hearing. Once there, I was asked to explain how I had been able to attend graduate school on a part-time basis. I had to explain my reasons for providing a home for a child who had been in foster care. In my opinion, I was required to justify why I had not given up on life the moment I had gotten sick.

The judge's decision would have an affect on my life but would not rule it. In some ways, the hearing was much easier than I expected. After the hearing was finished, I realized that I had been so upset that I forgot to mention many things that could have strengthened my case.

What really matters, though, is the knowledge that God is my judge. His righteousness has been transferred to me by the blood of Jesus Christ. Throughout the illness, God was my witness. I do not have to justify anything to Him. I trust Him. He knows me and understands that I did not want to be ill. God supplies my needs, not an insurance company or social security. To be judged by humans can be intimidating, but to be judged by God is mercy.

Have you struggled with insurance claims? What can you ask from God if you are required to document or justify your need for assistance?

_____

_____

_____

_____

_____

৵৶

For the message of the cross is foolishness to those who are
perishing, but to us who are being saved it is the power of God.
—1 CORINTHIANS 1:18

Because I was faced with daily responsibilities and trials, I did not keep my mind on the cross every moment. I wanted to, but distractions occurred. Distractions are sometimes inevitable for humans, but God does not become distracted. He remains aware and involved with His children at all times, even when He is not foremost in our thoughts. The Holy Spirit is with us every moment, and He helps us get our eyes back on Jesus.

Jesus' sacrifice for our sins brought a new covenant. Through the shedding of His blood, we gained the privilege of communicating directly with God. Those of us who give our hearts to God will not perish. Jesus' death on the cross provided a way for the souls of believers to live eternally in the presence of God. I thank God for the message He gives in His Word about the purpose of Jesus' blood and the cross. It covers my sins, not by hiding them, but by cleansing them from my soul. The cross has power over illness, despair, and death. Although Jesus' death occurred two thousand years ago, the cross continues to bear witness of God's love.

For an extended period of time, I was afraid that I would perish. Physical pain threatened to consume me. In His Word, God promises that the outward person may perish but the inward person would be renewed each day. I remember the desperate day that I asked God to prove this promise to me. I was helpless, but God provided His mercy. In the midst of my darkest moments, my spirit was renewed. I never again asked God to let me die. Instead of perishing, my spirit grew stronger. God's love remains my foundation.

The message of the cross is salvation, and through God's saving grace believers are continually renewed. As Christians, we demonstrate the power of the cross as we live in peace in spite of pain. Even if we are ill, our peace can serve as a powerful influence on unbelievers. Even through our pain, the Holy Spirit will help us pray for fellow Christians and unbelievers. As we pray for others, God renews us.

Although my body continued to have pain, I knew something better awaited me. At times, it seemed that physical healing would not occur. Pain could not stop my heart from soaring when I thought of eternal life, a life with God that has no pain or struggles. Lord, thank You for Jesus' sacrifice, the most beautiful and powerful gift that has ever been given.

Have you realized the life-changing power of the cross? How can the message of the cross help people with whom you have contact?

❧❧

And most of the brethren in the Lord, having become confident
by my chains, are much more bold to speak the word without fear.
—PHILIPPIANS 1:14

I have never been shackled with chains, but I have seen loved ones and former students enter courtrooms in restraints. My heart has broken every time I have seen someone I know in a shackled condition. The chains speak a clear and loud message, telling everyone who sees them that the bound individual is in trouble.

The most powerful chains, in my opinion, are those that are invisible. I was bound by the invisible chains of the enemy. Satan uses many types of burdens in his attempts to chain people's spirits. Chains form when illnesses, depression, family conflict, or financial stress overpowers a believer. The enemy has many more tools by which he attempts to arrest the spiritual growth of God's people.

I remember how it felt to be bound by the power of illness. The chains of trigeminal neuralgia held me captive in a prison of fear and dysfunction. Although I was imprisoned by pain and fear, God was faithful to me. He did not cast me aside or forget about me. When I decided to pursue God's will rather than my own, a healing process began.

Once I understood that it was the enemy's power that had stolen my freedom, I began to get angry. I was not angry with God anymore, and I was ready to fight in God's army against Satan. As God prepared me for victory, I grew stronger in His love and His Word. My faith also grew. I am not a person whom others would consider timid, but my boldness had not come from God. It was of my flesh, my own will. Now I continue to learn how to be bold in the Lord. With God's whole armor, I fought to break free from the binding chains of Satan's oppression. The more I fought, the stronger I got. My determination grew stronger with prayer.

I became proud to be a Spirit-filled woman. I am not afraid or ashamed to tell people why I decided to go to a little country church. Through a closer walk with Jesus, I had found joy and confidence. My relationship with God became the most important thing in my life. It became more important than whether or not I was experiencing pain. I had assurance that the wall of pain will one day fall down. Meanwhile, I continued to shout.

Has your illness caused you to feel as though you are imprisoned? How will God help you speak boldly about His love?

_____

_____

_____

_____

_____

❧❧❧

Chapter 7

Breaking the Yoke

For now I will break off his yoke from you,
And burst your bonds apart.

—NAHUM 1:13

In spite of my praises, pain remained constant and often severe. In early March of 2004, six years after the pains of trigeminal began, I was still suffering. For three consecutive nights, the pain raged. I got little sleep at night, and my efforts to nap during the day were futile. I felt extremely fatigued. I asked God for a good night's sleep. I told Him that I did not think I could continue one more day without sleep.

God answered my prayer. I got a good night's sleep, and when I awoke the following morning, I was not in pain. In fact, I did not have pain the entire day. Bedtime came before I realized that I had gone through the day without taking pain medication. I knew God had heard my prayer. I thanked Him for His mercy.

Once again, I slept through the night without any pain. The next morning, I was able to walk outside. I could groom myself without any difficulty. I talked clearly, and I called many of my friends to let them know that I was doing better. I talked about God's mercy to anyone who would listen. I knew that a heavy and terrible yoke had been broken. Through the blood of Jesus Christ, my bonds of illness shattered.

When harsh pain reoccurred, I learned to find a private place to worship God. Sometimes it was in the middle of a crowded room or in the privacy of my own car. At these times, my spirit connected with His, and I gained His assurance that the pain will not overcome me.

I wanted so desperately to rebuild my life. Although I could not endure much physical exercise, I was not at the starting point of my spiritual walk. My goal is to be a spiritual athlete, and God is my trainer. I have heard God's signal to proceed, and now it is time to run. I run to

God, not away from Him. Thank you, Lord, for breaking my bonds and setting my spirit free.

Have you felt as though you are bound by your illness? What bonds will you ask God to break?

_____

_____

_____

_____

_____

৵৵৵

Sing to Him, sing psalms to Him; Talk of all His wondrous works!
—1 Chronicles 16:9

During times of prolonged pain, Christian music soothed me and offered hope. Now that I began to have pain-free days, I rejoiced in my ability to sing along with the music. While so many songs provided me with encouragement, one song seemed to hold my testimony: "In Amazing Graceland." Written by Wayne Kirkpatrick and Phil Madeira, this song states the fact that healing is delivered through the love of God.

I began to practice this song with my friend Shelia, and I thanked God for the ability to sing, to be able to move my facial muscles. I thanked Him for relief from the pain. I knew I was healed. One morning after Shelia and I had practiced, the familiar pain returned to the right side of my face. The pain was bearable, and I knew that a person with advanced trigeminal neuralgia should not be attempting to sing. I decided that the best thing to do was to rest. I had pushed myself, and my doctor had advised me not to do that.

On the path to victory, people make mistakes. The decision to retreat was one of mine. It was not born from prayer but from looking at my situation through the eyes of medicine. When we look at our medical conditions through the eyes of science, we place limits on God. I did not understand that the enemy had come to test my faith. I was stepping out to sing God's praises, and Satan was not willing to admit defeat.

Because I have now learned more about God's healing virtue, I know that I should have continued to sing when I experienced symptoms. It was time to stand on the fact that God had delivered me from trigeminal neuralgia. Proclaiming victory through blood of Jesus, I could have continued singing God's praises. I could have avoided more torturous pain.

The previous weeks without pain became a distant memory as electrocution-type pains began to devour me once more. I felt more confused than ever. Although the pain was more frequent than ever, I refused to relinquish hope. I continued to serve God, and He remained faithful to me. Regardless of the circumstances, I knew that I lived "In Amazing Graceland."

Have you experienced trials when testifying about God's love? How have your praises helped you on your path to victory?

_____

_____

_____

_____

_____

❧❧❧

Sow for yourselves righteousness; Reap in mercy;
Break up your fallow ground, For it is time to seek the Lord,
Till He comes and rains righteousness on you.

—HOSEA 10:12

God proved His faithfulness in many ways, and I could see God's truths prevail in my life. I was willing to serve Him in spite of my pain. When my church needed a substitute Sunday school teacher, I always had a reprieve from the pain. I could concentrate enough to prepare and teach a lesson.

I am thankful to learn that everyone can contribute to God's kingdom. Although my contribution was not difficult, God showered His blessings on me. I began to experience even more of God's mercy. God's love rained upon me in spite of the fact that I did not deserve it. The essence of mercy is His love, and God loves us and blesses us because He is good. Mercy overlooks our failures and inconsistencies.

During the time that I was helping my church with Sunday school, four hurricanes ravaged Florida. Our home was in the projected path of three of the storms. Each time we were threatened by a hurricane, we had no choice but to prepare for the worst. Once we lost power for four hours. When our electricity came back on, I remember thanking God. Later I realized how inadequate my few words of praise were. Most people in our county and in the surrounding counties were without electricity for a minimum of four days. When I learned about the widespread outages, I realized how blessed we had been.

Each time a hurricane passed over us, I experienced trigeminal pain caused by changes in barometric pressure. Although I had pain, I was able to stay in my home. With my husband's help, I could prepare simple meals. Our air conditioner worked, and our water supply was not disturbed. Regardless of the turmoil around us and of the pain that I felt, our home remained our shelter. Once again, God's protection had guarded me from harm. When the storms came, God's righteous love rained on me. I saw His love in the clouds, I heard it in the wind, and

I felt it in drops of rain. I began to realize that healing—complete and everlasting—was on its way.

Have you experienced God's protection? How can the storms in your life provide reassurance of God's mercy?

_____

_____

_____

_____

_____

❧❧❧

But to you who fear My name The Sun of Righteousness shall
arise With healing in His wings; And you shall go out
And grow fat like stall-fed calves.

—MALACHI 4:2

As time passed, my spirit gained the assurance that healing was mine. Matthew 4:23–25 also speaks of Jesus' healing power. Christ healed people who had many different types of diseases. He healed those with paralysis, epilepsy, and those who were demon possessed. Jesus offers healing for others who would call on Him. I began to call even more passionately, and He answered me.

God has never spoken to me in an audible voice, yet my spirit recognizes His inaudible voice. One evening, I prayed in my family room, kneeling by the sofa. As I prayed, God began to speak to me. At the same time, an image flashed before me. I did not see it with my eyes, but I saw it within my own spirit. What I saw was my body, packaged in an invisible cylinder. My arms were by my sides. Outside this cylinder were evil forces. They had their hands placed on the cylinder, but they could not penetrate it. Inside I remained protected.

The image was fleeting, and as soon as it disappeared, I asked God what it meant. My spirit, not my ears, heard His voice. You have a few more valleys to endure, and then you will be healed. My entire body seemed to cry. I was not happy at the idea of experiencing more valleys. Then I realized that I had to cling to the affirmation that healing was on its way. The affirmation began to grow, and soon I realized my spirit had been strengthened as I walked through a valley of pain. I had drawn closer to God, and I had learned how to walk in faith and in God's mercy.

One of the most wonderful things about this prayer is that God spoke to me in a unique way. In a fleeting moment, He reassured me that He was protecting me from the enemy. God was keeping His word: I would not perish. One day I would be healthy and strong again, just like the stall-fed calves.

Do you believe that healing awaits you? How does your relationship with God help you build your faith?

_____

_____

_____

_____

_____

৯৵৶৶

Not that I have already attained, or am already perfected;
but I press on, that I may lay hold of that for which
Christ Jesus has also laid hold of me.
—PHILIPPIANS 3:12

Knowing that complete healing awaited me, I began to pursue God even more fervently. I had become quite frustrated by my situation. I was in pain almost all the time. Pain awakened me in the morning. One night as I prayed at the altar at church, God spoke to my spirit again: *I am going to take you to a higher place.* I knew what God wanted. He wanted me to step up to a higher place spiritually so that I could receive my healing. It was time to let go of things I could not control and focus totally on Jesus.

I have never been good at letting things go. I tend to thoroughly analyze situations, others, and myself. This takes a lot of energy, and healing required all the energy I could muster. Physically, I had grown quite weak. I did not have enough stamina for anger or worry, yet I often worried. Sometimes I became angry too. I tried to shut my husband out of my life. His life was still full, and he was able to go out of town for sports events and other activities. I felt trapped inside my body, and every time my husband left our home it reminded me that I was not able to go with him. Like people who become accustomed to life in prison, I began to allow the bonds of illness to ensnare me.

I realized that my outlook was flawed when I once again felt the chains that can accompany illness. The Word gives us clear evidence that Jesus came to free us. In Matthew 8:32, Jesus' words tell us that we will know the truth and that the truth will make us free. Did I know the truth? Absolutely! I knew that Jesus Christ is the Son of God. He sacrificed His life to offer me eternal life. I had accepted salvation, and I was free in spite of the pain. It was time to press in, time to act like a woman who had freedom instead of restrictions.

The Holy Spirit impressed me to choose a particular time and place to receive my healing. I asked the Holy Spirit for a divine appointment with Him. My family and friends offered prayers and support. Soon my frustrations and anger began to fade. I began to claim victory in the Lord. I chose an anticipated date for my healing. I prayed about going to a healing service, and God confirmed that I should attend. The event was almost two months away. The pain continued to rage, but I knew that it would soon end. Although my healing was not perfected, it was definitely in sight.

Have you longed to press in to the healing power of Jesus? How can you focus more specifically on your healing?

_____

_____

_____

_____

_____

❧❧

The heart of the wise is in the house of mourning.

—ECCLESIASTES 7:4

Many times in life, I have asked God for wisdom. One area in which I have needed wisdom is in building friendships. Many times I have placed faith in someone who was not loyal, and later I would be hurt simply because I had invested in a friendship that I had not asked God to bless or approve. As I matured, I began to ask God to teach me how to recognize true friends.

Years earlier as I became acquainted with my sister-in-law Peggy, I knew that I had found a true friend. Three weeks before my anticipated day of healing arrived, my husband and I learned that Peggy was in the final days of her life. Less than a year had passed since we learned that she had liver cancer. We began to make trips to her hospital room and then to her home.

As we commuted to Peggy's home, I thought of the weekly overnight trips to her home. I had spent many nights with Peggy and my brother-in-law, Herb, when I attended graduate courses in counseling. Although Peggy and Herb were providing me with a place to spend the night, Peggy always acted as though she was the person who was being blessed rather than the person providing the blessing. On those nights, she spread a blanket of hospitality and friendship that was unmatched. I cherished each moment with her and Herb, and I thanked God for giving me such wonderful family. My husband and Herb are brothers, and this special blessing had come through marriage.

Before I learned of Peggy's illness, I recognized the love Peggy and Herb had for each other. Their love exuded comfort, and they succeeded in bestowing their love upon others. I had begun to work on *With Great Mercy* before Peggy's cancer was diagnosed. When I learned about her situation, I asked Peggy if she would like to read the entries I had written. As she read the entries, she encouraged me to continue. One day when I visited her, she showed me a file she had created for the entries. Peggy voiced her appreciation.

Sometimes I feel so unworthy and inadequate. I felt inadequate as a friend and sister because Peggy's love continued to bless me when my desire was to be the giver. Peggy always managed to return love and to support others. My husband and I were determined to be with her in her final days. My pain seemed irrelevant and minor compared to the trauma her husband, daughters, and son experienced. As I approached the day I had claimed for my healing, I lost one of the best friends and best sisters anyone could have. I thank God for Peggy, and I am so grateful that God helped me recognize how blessed I was to have her friendship and her love.

Do you need a special family member or friend as you find your path to healing? How will you recognize the blessings He has made ready for you?

_____

_____

_____

_____

_____

❧❧

Chapter 8

A Walk in the Spirit

And those who are Christ's have crucified the
flesh with its passions and desires. If we live in the Spirit,
let us also walk in the Spirit.

—GALATIANS 5:24–25

My family reunion was scheduled just a day or so after Peggy's death. The reunion was only an hour's drive from our home. Bob and I were tired, and I was experiencing unrelenting facial pain. We knew that the following two days would also be spent away from home for Peggy's memorial services, yet the opportunity to see our family compelled us to go.

When I arrived at the reunion, I saw a couple of individuals I never expected to be there. Upon seeing them, anger and emotional pain stirred afresh in my heart. I walked over to them with the purpose of asking them why they had been so cruel. As I took the steps toward them, something happened to me. The Holy Spirit touched my heart, my spirit. I remembered how much I loved the two family members. Instead of confronting them about their behavior, I hugged them the way I would have hugged Peggy if I had another chance. I told them I loved them, and I meant it.

When we returned home, I rested for the two days of activity ahead. The following morning, I felt quite rested. I began to brush my teeth and was pierced by the most severe torture I have ever experienced. Electrocution-type pains entered from my jaw and exploded into my ear. Fresh pains came every second, and I could do nothing but scream. Immediately my husband was behind me, holding me so that I would not collapse. After the intense pains subsided, he helped me into bed. Grief flooded my heart because I knew I would not be able to attend the services to honor my sister-in-law. She spent her life honoring others, and I desired one last chance to honor her.

My husband did not want to leave me alone, but no other choice existed. My family and friends were in church because it was Sunday morning. Bob's family was out of town preparing for the memorial services. Bob offered to stay with me, but we both knew that he needed to be with his brother. I knew that I needed something special from God if I were to endure the afternoon alone. I was not able to read, so I asked Bob to play Mel Gibson's *The Passion of the Christ*. I had seen the movie several times, and for me the film is a visual reminder of Jesus' love. When the movie began to show the beating that Jesus took for the healing of His people, I began to experience a power surge in my spirit. I sat up in bed. For the first time, I watched this portion of the movie without crying. This scene empowered me; it confirmed my healing. I claimed victory over trigeminal neuralgia and the enemy's plan to destroy me.

My spirit reached out for Jesus' healing power and did not turn back. The day of my appointed healing was only two weeks away. No pain the enemy inflicted could convince me otherwise. I knew the Lord had taken me to a higher place through His mercy and love. I was ready to receive my healing.

Have you encountered a situation that required you to relinquish anger or emotional pain? When has the Holy Spirit provided you with strength beyond your own capabilities?

_____

_____

_____

_____

_____

❧❧❧

Examine yourselves as to whether you are in the faith.
Test yourselves. Do you not know yourselves, that Jesus Christ
is in you?—unless indeed you are disqualified.

—2 Corinthians 13:5

Every time that I had been hit with such tremendous pain, a month or more of torture would follow. The time had come to exercise my faith. Within a couple of days, I was out of bed. Pain remained, but the severity of it had lessened. I believed that if I did not have the faith to continue with daily activities that I would not have the faith to receive my healing. God's faithfulness proved to be evident. A friend came to stay with me for several days. I was reassured to have someone with me rather than to be alone. I also had a visit from my aunt who told me how God had healed her of a debilitating neurological disorder.

I searched my heart and my mind for doubt or unbelief. I realized that I had surrendered to pain when I had begun to sing "In Amazing Graceland." The opportunity to sing still existed, and Shelia and I began to practice once more. I remembered all the times my speaking had been distorted by trigeminal neuralgia. I would not have agreed to speak at the front of a church, so the thought of singing was even more intimidating. For almost seven years I lacked the security that I would be able to project my voice or hold a note. Now the time had come for me to test my faith.

Exactly one week before the date I had marked for my healing, Shelia and I sang "In Amazing Graceland" in our church. It proved to be one of my most emotional experiences. I had to trust God every time I opened my mouth to sing a note. My desire to sing was to issue the message of God's grace and not to bring attention to myself, yet I would have been terribly embarrassed if a pain forced me to stop singing.

Most of the people in the church that night did not know my circumstances. They were unaware that I had to trust God for every syllable, for every note. What I remember the most is singing this line: "Without Your love, there would be no healing." God helped me sing without pain.

He had given me the desire and strength to step out in faith. I had to be certain that I would trust in Jesus Christ when I was put to a test. I had sung my testimony, and my spirit felt the walls of Jericho begin to crumble.

Have you avoided engaging in a form of worship because your symptoms might occur? How can an exercise of faith increase your strength?

_____

_____

_____

_____

_____

❧❧

Surely He shall deliver you from the snare of the fowler
and from the perilous pestilence.... You shall not be afraid of the
terror by night, Nor of the arrow that flies by day.

—PSALM 91:3, 5

A *week passed quickly.* My anticipated date of healing had arrived. Now I walked from a hotel room to an arena where a healing crusade was to be held. I was with my mother and two friends from church. As we got closer to the building, my symptoms grew worse. Someone stopped to ask me a question, and the electrocution-type pains began to rivet through my head. I looked at my mother and told her that I would not talk anymore until I got into the building.

The afternoon was warm with a slight breeze. I wrapped my black scarf around my face because the breeze triggered pains. At one point, two young ladies noticed that I was in distress. They asked if they could help us pray. I will never forget them. Then we found the door to which we had been assigned entrance. I looked back at the hotel and remembered how almost seven years earlier I had awakened there during the night. My sleep had been disturbed with pain that I would come to know as trigeminal neuralgia. My husband and I had traveled to another city without understanding the gravity of my situation. Since that night almost seven years earlier, I often remembered awakening there, experiencing pain and panic.

As my thoughts returned to present events, I noticed a gentleman standing next to me. He attempted to engage in polite conversation, but I told him that talking caused pain. He apologized and respected my desire to remain silent. One of the ladies with me asked him if he were a minister, and the gentleman gave her his business card. Then someone near me made a shocking statement: "You are a neurosurgeon!"

The neurosurgeon stood next to me. I immediately turned to him and stated my case: "I have trigeminal neuralgia." He had seen the scarf around my face and had insight regarding its purpose. We began to talk, and he asked if he could pray for me. Over the years, many people have

127

prayed for me, some with powerful anointing. Yet no one had really understood the architecture of my nervous system, and the neurosurgeon named the nerve, addressed the condition, and asked God to perform a creative miracle. Standing outside a building, the Spirit of God poured out heaven's mercy, and my miracle began. My entire body began to shake. When I opened my eyes, people were respectfully observing. I believe they sensed God's presence.

The enemy had tried to defeat me as the hour of my healing drew close, yet God sent a man who was both a neurosurgeon and a minister to stand beside me. Although Satan's arrows were aimed in my direction, God used one of His servants to help me escape them. My precious Lord sent a member of His army to help me stand and to assure me of deliverance. I no longer had to look to the future for healing. I looked back at the hotel again. I had stayed in it two nights, almost seven years apart. During my first stay, I had been frightened by pain from the early stages of trigeminal neuralgia. I had also stayed the previous night, fearing nothing. After seven years, the healing virtue of Jesus Christ brought me out of the terror by night.

Has the enemy attempted to terrify you as you have stepped out in faith? Whom will you ask to stand with you as you approach victory?

_____

_____

_____

_____

_____

But now, O Lord, You are our Father; We are the clay, and
You our potter; And all we are the work of Your hand.
—ISAIAH 64:8

Inside the convention center, thousands of people had gathered to
receive and witness miracles. As I waited for the service to begin,
spiritual warfare continued. I knew that I had just experienced God's
power, yet my flesh compelled me to ask God to confirm my healing.
For weeks I had expected to be healed *inside* the building. My prayers
had been specific. I had asked God to allow me to feel the warmth of the
Holy Spirit as I was healed, and I asked Him for trigeminal neuralgia to
be named as a condition that was being healed. I had formulated a plan,
and I expected God to follow it.

On October 24, 2004, I sat in the midst of a healing crusade with full
knowledge that the pastor could not heal me. I did not understand why
God's plan required me to travel to another city and to encounter an
enormous crowd. On this night I learned that God follows His plans and
not mine. I also learned that I sometimes become so involved in my own
expectations that I do not see God's work in my life.

When the corporate prayer for healing began, the pain in my face
raged once more. Doubt crept in. I remembered the healing power that
touched my body outside the building. Now I wondered why again I
felt the presence of God and the pain in my face at the same time. Then
the pastor asked people to place their hands on the part of the body
that needed healing. I placed my hand on the right side of my face, and
my spirit continued to cry out to God. I heard the pastor ask us to do
something we could not do before, so I opened up my mouth as widely
as possible. For the first time in almost seven years, not only could I
open my mouth widely, but I also felt no pain as I attempted this.

My body became very limp, and I remember my mother holding me
in her arms. While my mother held me, I heard the pastor say that someone was being healed of terrible headaches. In silent prayers I pleaded
with God to allow me to feel the warmth of His healing power and to

hear "trigeminal neuralgia." As I waited to feel the warmth and to hear the two words, I became agitated. Then I realized I could not deny the fact that the Holy Spirit's power had descended on me. Suddenly it no longer mattered how God healed me because I knew, I really knew, that my healing was complete.

Do you expect God to provide healing in a specific manner? How can you become more sensitive to God's Spirit?

_____

_____

_____

_____

_____

❧❦

But the God of all grace, who hath called us unto his eternal
glory by Christ Jesus, after that ye have suffered a while,
make you perfect, stablish, strengthen, settle you.

—1 Peter 5:10, kjv

As my mother and I approached the floor of the arena, I thanked
God that my healing was complete. It had begun in my uncle's
church more than a year earlier, and God had sent the neurosurgeon to
pray for me outside the building. It seemed that nothing could quench
my desire for further confirmation from the Lord. I am so thankful that
God did not become angry with me. Instead He poured out a double
portion of Jesus' healing mercy. Near the platform, I was totally overwhelmed by the presence of God. When a physician asked me how I
knew I was healed, I could barely remember my symptoms. I began to
show him what I could do that I could not do before.

I prayed fervently as my mother and I approached the platform. I did
not want to speak because I felt so emotional, yet I wanted to testify. I
wanted to be an instrument of hope to anyone with trigeminal neuralgia.
When I was led onto the platform, someone announced that I had been
healed of trigeminal neuralgia. Then the pastor mentioned the severe
headaches. He also spoke of the pain he saw "going through" my head
and asked me to explain its nature. Just a few moments later, my mother
and I were led off the platform. Soon we were on our way home.

I fell asleep so easily that night. In the early hours of the morning,
I was awakened by pain in my face. The pain was not the electrocution-type of pain, but it was the stabbing pain that is typical of atypical
trigeminal neuralgia. The first thing I thought about was that the neurosurgeon had told me that no symptom could take my healing from me.
He had advised me to ignore them and to continue to praise God for my
healing. I commanded the enemy to leave in the name of Jesus. Then I
went right back to sleep.

The next day, I had more symptoms, but they never increased to
the point of "electrocution" pains. I stayed in my home for several days

because I wanted to be alone with God. I prayed almost constantly because I could not thank Him enough. I read F. F. Bosworth's book, *Christ the Healer*. It helped me understand that my healing had been waiting for me. Through prayer and reading the Bible, I began to understand the significance of the apostle Paul's message in 1 Corinthians 13:12, "For now we see through a glass, darkly" (KJV). I finally understood what I had not previously grasped. My healing was provided long before my faith was strong enough to accept it.

Every day my healing becomes a more powerful part of who I am. I have not taken a pain pill since October 23, 2004. I will always be grateful that prescription pain medicines were available to help me cope with the pain, but I am happy to be free of pain medication. I am now also free of symptoms. I am free because I was healed—not in a church, not outside a building, not inside a healing service. I was healed in Jerusalem more than 2000 years ago. Jesus Christ endured a flogging so that I could be healed. He died on a cross so that I could be saved.

Has your understanding of God's mercy been strengthened?
How does a greater understanding God's love build your faith?

_____

_____

_____

_____

_____

It is good for me that I have been afflicted,
That I may learn your statutes.

—PSALM 119:71

The only good thing about having trigeminal neuralgia is that I learned to depend upon God in ways I had not previously imagined. All quality of life was stolen by the enemy, and I did not understand how my condition could have positive results. In Romans 8:28, the Word of God states that all things work together for the good of those who love God and are called for His purpose. After years of confusion and then years of seeking God's mercy, I began to understand how my pain could result in something positive.

Since the onset of trigeminal neuralgia, I yearned for God's Spirit to touch me with complete and instantaneous healing. For me, healing is a walk of faith, a daily process. Healing also involves secondary situations that occurred as a result of an extended illness. Because managing the pain took most of my abilities, I relinquished my other responsibilities. My husband and my mother managed my household. For me, healing includes learning how to cope with responsibilities. Many days hold significant challenges as I learn to concentrate again. To become an independent person again, I must tackle things that initially seem difficult. Being healthy and whole makes the challenge worthwhile.

My desire is to grow closer and closer to God. I will always remember that God was faithful as I traveled through a valley of torment. He sent others to help me. When I had trigeminal neuralgia, I learned what faithfulness is. I learned that God's love fills us, allowing us to care for one another. Although I experienced many losses while I was ill, my husband, my mother, and my closest friends remained faithful to me. My uncle and aunt never turned me away when I walked to the front of the church for prayer.

The experience of having trigeminal neuralgia has helped me appreciate things that I did not appreciate as a healthy person. I hate violent pain, and I will never accept it as a normal part of my life. I will never accept it as God's will. Yet the only effective cure I have found is to walk with the Lord as a daily experience. Now my relationship with Him does not grow hot and cold at my convenience. God taught me how to be faithful to Him as He faithfully provides all my needs according to His riches in heaven.

Have you wondered if anything good can result from your illness? How can you learn more about God while you wait for His answer?

_____

_____

_____

_____

_____

❧❧

If any of you lacks wisdom, let him ask of God, who gives to all
liberally and without reproach, and it will be given to him.

—JAMES 1:5

Now that I have received my healing, I have many decisions to
make. My future is uncertain. Seven years ago, I was unaware of
how quickly life can change. Today I have a keen awareness that sur-
prises may come with each new day. I do not fear the future, and I have
a strong desire to be in the center of God's will. I pray, yet I know that
I should pray more. I want to experience more of God's presence, His
blessings, His mercy, and His wisdom.

I am so glad that God promises to give wisdom to those who ask for it.
I do not want my future to be like my past, when I was tossed easily by the
strong winds of life. I know I am responsible for some of the strong winds
that blew me about. They came because I pursued my own desires rather
than the path that God had set before me. Now that I walk on God's path,
I sometimes hear the strong winds howl. Through my trust in God, my
foot remains firmly planted, and I am not tossed about. My spirit and my
faith continue to become stronger.

Staying on the path which God designed for me requires me to be
in touch with Him. Sometimes my prayers are answered immediately,
and at other times I must wait for an answer. Waiting requires wisdom.
Although I have matured in my ability to wait for God, my flesh still
wants to race ahead with my own desires. That is when I need God's
wisdom the most.

One of my desires is to finish my master's degree. I am close to
achieving this goal, but I realize that I pursued my studies at my own
detriment. I continued taking classes until my body refused to cooper-
ate. From loading myself with too many responsibilities, I learned that I
need to make God my highest priority. I will wait until I am physically
stronger before I attempt to return to school. I will also wait to be sure
that it is part of God's plan for my life. In the meantime, I thank God for
giving me opportunities to testify.

As a student in the counseling field, I have learned how important it is for each of us to tell our own stories. It gives us an opportunity to examine the results of our pain and to realize that we have not given in to despair. Our spirits survive. I did not plan to take a break from my studies, yet God has blessed me marvelously during the break. I have had more time for God, and I have received greater peace through my time spent in prayer. Lord, thank You for offering wisdom to your people. Please do not let me forget that I need to pray about my decisions.

Do you need wisdom to help you make an important decision? How can wisdom from God help you improve your quality of life?

_____

_____

_____

_____

_____

❧❧

The Spirit of the Lord is upon Me, Because He has anointed Me
To preach the gospel to the poor; He has sent Me to
heal the brokenhearted, To proclaim liberty to the captives
And recovery of sight to the blind, To set at
liberty those who are oppressed.

—LUKE 4:18

God's love and healing are complete. For several years I wanted physical healing, but God wanted to accomplish a complete work. I just wanted a shortcut. God knew what I really needed, and it was much more than the decompression of my trigeminal nerve. I needed trust, hope, and joy. I needed emotional healing because I was hurt by some people's lack of understanding and disbelief of my pain. These hurtful situations had scarred my inner being.

The son of God became flesh, and Jesus was born to deliver a mighty message to all humans. God loves us whether we are rich or poor, happy or brokenhearted, free or imprisoned. Poverty, sadness, disabilities, and imprisonment might diminish a person's value in the eyes of the world, but God loves and understands each of us. Although we have difficulty loving ourselves, God has no difficulty in loving us. In 1 John 4:8, the Bible clearly states that "God is love." Because He loves us, God wants to restore our bodies, our lives, and our spirits.

The blood of Jesus provides restoration. Jesus' life, death, and resurrection prove His willingness to experience pain. They also testify of His ability to overcome pain and death. Jesus wants to release us from despair. His Father made us, and God knows our potential. We can reach our full potential only by giving our hearts to God.

I want God to help me reach my full potential. I want to remain free from the bonds of illness. I want to have God's riches, which far exceed the materialism of this world. I want to keep my joy because it provides me with inner peace even when I am experiencing rejection and conflict. I do not feel guilty or greedy for these desires because Jesus came to fulfill them. If I do not reach out for these gifts, then I do not allow myself to receive what God intended for me to have.

The miracle of Jesus' sacrifice sustains me on a daily basis. Although I am filled with the Holy Spirit, I remain flesh. Often I am weak, and I tire easily. When I have not had enough sleep, I display my emotions more than I prefer. I have weaknesses, but God knows my heart and sees my potential. My flaws do not diminish my Lord's love for me. The Holy Spirit remains with me every second of every day to protect and comfort me. I will always need to draw close to God because I am made whole through His love.

Have you ever focused on receiving only part of God's blessings?
How can you become whole through God's complete love?

_____

_____

_____

_____

_____

৵৵

Oh, give thanks to the Lord, for He is good!
For His mercy endures forever.

—PSALM 107:1

Regardless of what I do or say, I will never be able to prove to others how thankful I am for God's mercy. My actions do not always testify the extent of my love for God, but I am glad that He knows my heart. He knows that I will never be able to thank Him enough for His blessings. God freely rewards me with His favor, and in return He wants my love. Now I know how it feels to be gathered into God's merciful arms. Perfect peace comes over my spirit, and the circumstances of life become irrelevant. My spirit is renewed, and I have the resources to press forward in my walk of faith. God removes my fears, and He gives me the boldness to speak His word.

I have witnessed God's magnificent faithfulness. My ability to love and trust Him grew tremendously as I walked through the valley of pain. Before I became ill, I did not ask for His comfort. I believed that He had helped me become a strong individual and that I could depend on myself. Through the torment, I learned to trust God with my mind and my heart. He knew the extent of my suffering and reached down to help me when I could not help myself. I have learned of His mercy, and God's love has become my solace.

I remember hearing so often that trigeminal neuralgia is the "suicide disease." Although I never entertained the idea of suicide, many times I asked God to swiftly take me on to heaven. I did not believe that I could bear the pain any longer. I am so glad that God helped me live through the pain. I know that God came to my side even during my worst despair. I praise God for the scriptures that have come alive from His Word. These scriptures have renewed my spirit, and God's love has given me joy.

I would have never chosen to endure the physical pain of trigeminal neuralgia. If someone had told me that I could tolerate this type of suffering, I would not have believed it. God has lifted me up in the midst of intense torment, and I have learned what it means to fight the good fight of faith and to reach out for God's mercy. Through this process, the concept of eternal life has become a reality. Heaven is not a fairy tale. Hell is not a science-fiction movie.

God's love and the power of the cross is the life-changing message that all believers are responsible for demonstrating in their lives. We deliver this message to others if we keep our peace in the midst of walking through fires. God's great mercy provides us with the stamina to continue, even when we do not understand how we can go on. I did not ask for a testimony, yet God gave me one through His power and truth.

Lord, I thank you for your love and mercy. I praise you for sending Jesus, who carried my sins. I ask you to bless others with your healing power and to give them perfect love and peace.

Has God given you a testimony? How can your pain result in winning others to Christ?

_____

_____

_____

_____

_____

❧❧